VINAIGRETTES
AND OTHER DRESSINGS

Other Books by
MICHELE ANNA JORDAN

The World Is a Kitchen

VegOut! Vegetarian Guide to San Francisco Bay Area

The BLT Cookbook

San Francisco Seafood

The New Cook's Tour of Sonoma

Pasta Classics

Salt & Pepper

California Home Cooking

Polenta

Pasta with Sauces

Ravioli & Lasagne

*The Good Cook's Book of Days:
A Food Lover's Journal*

The Good Cook's Book of Tomatoes

The Good Cook's Book of Mustard

The Good Cook's Book of Oil & Vinegar

A Cook's Tour of Sonoma

VINAIGRETTES
AND OTHER DRESSINGS

60 SENSATIONAL RECIPES *to* LIVEN UP GREENS, GRAINS, SLAWS, *and* EVERY KIND *of* SALAD

MICHELE ANNA JORDAN

THE HARVARD COMMON PRESS
BOSTON, MASSACHUSETTS

The Harvard Common Press
www.harvardcommonpress.com

Printed in China
Printed on acid-free paper

Library of Congress Cataloging-in-Publication Data
Jordan, Michele Anna.
  Vinaigrettes and other dressings : 60 sensational recipes to liven up
greens, grains, slaws, and every kind of salad / Michele Anna Jordan.
    pages   cm
  Includes index.
  ISBN 978-1-55832-805-1
  1. Vinaigrettes. 2. Salad dressing. 3. Cookbooks. lcgft I. Title.
  TX819.S27J67 2013
  641.81'4--dc23
                              2012035547

Special bulk-order discounts are available on this and other Harvard
Common Press books. Companies and organizations may purchase
books for premiums or resale, or may arrange a custom edition, by
contacting the Marketing Director at the address above.

Book design by Deborah Kerner
Front cover photography by Joyce Oudkerk Pool
Text and back cover/spine photography by Kimberley Hasselbrink
Food styling by Michele Anna Jordan

10 9 8 7 6 5 4 3 2 1

For Patrick Bouquet,

you're the closest I've ever come to having a brother, in good times and bad, yours and mine. And no one shouts *"Fire!"* as effectively as you, Pati'o, even when it's just a muskrat under the slicer.

And for my sweet grandson, Lucas,

whose eager and adventurous palate has been an inspiration since his first baby-bird-like bite of solid food—K & L Bistro's cauliflower soup with black olive tapenade—at just six months of age. All the recipes with anchovies, feta, and blue cheese are for you, Lucas.

Contents

CHAPTER 4 Sassy *and* Spirited
Salads to Enjoy All Year 132

Acknowledgments

It has been a joy working with The Harvard Common Press. Dan Rosenberg, Valerie Cimino, Virginia Downes, Pat Jalbert-Levine, Jane Dornbusch, and Annabelle Blake: Y'all rock! And Bruce Shaw, thanks for this opportunity and for being so awesomely savvy about publishing in the age of iPads, Kindles, and social media.

And to my uber-brilliant agent, Andy Ross, thanks for smoothing the way on contractual stuff and for making me laugh. A lot.

As always, I am grateful to the farmers and ranchers of Sonoma County, who make my life so easy. Whether it's a head of butter lettuce, a succulent peach, a voluptuous egg, a juicy rack of lamb, or delicious olive oil, the foods of this special place are among the finest anywhere. I am also deeply indebted to the hardworking managers of our farmers' markets, who constantly endeavor to keep the best of our region's harvest available to the community. And I raise a glass of something bright and sparkling to our grape growers and winemakers, who help make the end of every day a celebration.

Many thanks to Kimberley Hasselbrink, who did a great job with photography. And special thanks to Gayle Sullivan of Dry Creek Peach and Produce for help during the photo shoot and, always, for the Arctic Gem white peaches. Thanks, as well, to Dominique Cortara of Dominique's Sweets for the surprise visit and yummy things to eat and drink that sustained us during shooting and clean up.

I send a big *mahalo nui loa* to my teacher Kumu Hula Shawna Alapa'i, my hula sisters, and singer Faith Ako for keeping my spirit well fed.

A special thank you goes to Rosemary McCune, hula sister, friend, confidante, co-conspirator, doggy sitter, and all-around cool *chica*. Rosemary was a great help with last-minute shopping ("Oops, the fennel died") and prep during the book's photo shoot.

To my beloved friend and landlady, Mary Duryee, and Joanne Derbort, my editor at the *Santa Rosa Press Democrat*, thank you from the deepest recesses of my heart.

Finally, to my dear friends John Boland and James Carroll, my daughters Gina and Nicolle, my grandson, Lucas, and my son-in-law, Tom, thank you for putting up with how busy I always seem to be. No matter what I am doing, I would always prefer to be around a table with all of you, talking, laughing, and sharing a great big salad.

Have a Salad…

A green salad, I firmly believe, should follow the main course of a meal, at noon or night, and should be made almost always and almost solely of fresh crisp garden lettuces tossed at the last with a plain vinaigrette."

—M. F. K. Fisher, from "One Way to Stay Young"
in *With Bold Knife and Fork* (1969)

From a few leaves of just-picked lettuces damp with an evening's rain and a creamy frenzy of earthy potatoes napped in a velvety mayonnaise to a cool mound of silky rice noodles in a tart and fiery dressing, salads delight and nourish us every day, the world round. Salads keep us healthy, happy, and alive.

In the past several decades, salads in America have improved in myriad delicious ways, with a huge variety of greens now available in supermarkets where, not that long ago, you might have found—if you were lucky to live in a sophisticated area—romaine lettuce alongside heads of iceberg. Now there's arugula, frisée and other heirloom chicories, spring salad mix, fall salad mix, tender butter lettuces, and more, all within easy reach of almost anyone. Who's eating them? Everyone. If they didn't sell, they wouldn't be there.

Our very definition of salad has been transformed, too, with almost everything we eat—save, say, chocolate and ice cream—making its way under that broad umbrella. Any fruit and vegetable can be found in a salad somewhere, as can grains like rice, farro, barley, and quinoa; pasta of every variety, shape, and size; various soft and hard cheeses; quail, chicken, duck, and turkey eggs; chicken, duck, quail, lamb, pork, beef, and bison; and all manner of fish and shellfish. Add a tangy vinaigrette or dollop of aioli and, *voilà*, salad!

Commercial salad dressings have expanded similarly, though I don't greet this development with the same enthusiasm as I do the proliferation of leafy greens. For the most part, commercial salad dressings eclipse rather than enhance the foods they cloak. They mask poorly grown greens and out-of-season tomatoes, but they don't enliven foods grown in their own time and harvested at their peak of flavor. These salad dressings, laden with salt, sugar, fat, and chemicals, may make swallowing vegetables easier for those who don't (or think they don't) like them, but they don't enrich the experience of those who love vegetables and seek out the best.

If I were Queen of the World, the supermarket shelves devoted to salad dressings would be emptied.

Of course, I am not, and so you have this book, my attempt to change the world one person at a time by convincing each and every one of you to wean yourself from commercial dressings and embrace the simple, delicious, thrifty, and healthful joy of making your own salad dressings. It takes a small bit of effort to achieve a huge payoff: delicious salads, every day.

A HAPPY PANTRY

A well-stocked pantry needn't include a comprehensive array of ingredients that rivals your local gourmet shop. It should simply contain everything you need to cook as you like to cook. Focus on high-quality brands of those items you actually use; add new ones as you discover, like, and understand them; and store them in a way that maintains their quality for as long as possible, which is to say in a cool cupboard away from sunlight, dampness, and heat from a stove, fireplace, or furnace. That's it.

These are the items I consider essential to making excellent salad dressings without having to run to the store.

GARLIC, SHALLOTS, AND ONIONS: Aromatics, as these ingredients are called, are essential in salad dressings, and it is important to buy the best and store them properly. Look first to local farmers' markets and farm stands and next to the organic section of your supermarket. Buy domestic items (not, say, garlic from China) that have been stored at room temperature if possible. Once you get these items home, do not put them in the refrigerator, which will destroy their flavors and textures. Instead, store in a cool, dry pantry. Never store potatoes nearby, as potatoes and aromatics each give off gasses that hasten the spoilage of the other.

HERBS: Herbs are almost always best used fresh. If you have room for even the smallest garden—a few pots on a front step or windowsill will work—grow those herbs you use most often. Recipes, especially for salad dressings, often call for a very small amount of an herb, and it's a waste to buy an entire bunch when you need only a few leaves. It is much more practical—and more flavorful—to walk outside and pick what you need. I always have chives, Italian parsley, thyme, oregano, marjoram, sage, and rosemary in my garden and sometimes have basil, cilantro, chervil, tarragon, and summer savory. If you must substitute dried herbs in a recipe, use no more than one-half the amount of fresh herbs that are called for; dried herbs should be replaced after six months.

HONEY: Honey is not, or should not be, a substitute for sugar, as it has its own distinct flavors. In salad dressings, it contributes complexity and depth as well as sweetness. For the best quality and flavor, look for organic raw honey produced close to where you live. Beekeeping is increasingly popular in the United States, and many small producers sell their honey at farmers' markets.

LEMONS: I consider lemons essential and I am rarely, if ever, without them. Look for them at farmers' markets, farm stands, and even the trees of friends and neighbors if you live in the right climate, before purchasing them at a supermarket, where they are generally overpriced. If you have a bounty of lemons, juice them, pour the juice into ice cube trays, and when the juice is frozen, pack the cubes in freezer bags. The juice from half a lemon should make about one standard-size cube. Juice from Meyer lemons, sweeter and less acidic than that from the ubiquitous Eureka lemon, can be frozen, too. If you need lemon zest, it's much easier to remove it from the lemon before cutting the fruit in half.

OLIVE OIL: Olive oil, especially olive oil that is produced mechanically without chemicals, is gentle on the environment, both of the earth and of the individual. For these reasons, along with its myriad pleasing flavors, it is the best default oil. You need a minimum of two olive oils in your pantry for making salad dressings: a premium extra-virgin olive oil with a flavor you love and a mild extra-virgin olive oil for general purposes, when a bold flavor may not be appropriate. Sometimes, olive oil without the "extra-virgin" designation is fine, especially in recipes that call for a mild-tasting oil. If you use a lot of olive oil in your cooking, it makes good sense—especially money-wise—to have both extra-virgin olive oils and ordinary olive oils on hand.

The fresher an oil is, the better it tastes. Look for oils that include the date of harvest on the label. Both light and heat are enemies of oil; make sure your oils are either packed in dark glass or, if bottled in clear glass, are in protective boxes. They should always be stored in a cool area.

Volumes have been written about contemporary olive oil. I tackled the topic in my second book, *The Good Cook's Book of Oil & Vinegar* (Perseus Books, 1992). The first California olive harvest following its publication ushered in a domestic renaissance, rendering most of what I had written about olive oil in my home state irrelevant. I had boldly declared that California olive oils were very good but not great. Then, one by one, new producers, harvesting from either long-neglected olive groves they had restored or new plantings of Italian varietals, proved me very wrong. Today, California olive oils are among the finest and most consistent in the world. I have my personal favorites, but there are many delicious olive oils produced today in California. The best way to explore them, other than to live there or visit, is to find a knowledgeable retailer near you or online.

OTHER OILS: I keep small bottles of expeller-pressed hazelnut oil and walnut oil in my refrigerator because I like their flavors; these oils are fragile and should be used within six months. To make salad dressings with authentic Asian flavors, you'll also need a bottle of toasted sesame oil, which is more shelf stable than nut oils and can be stored in the cupboard.

I do not use and do not recommend canola oil or grapeseed oil, in part because processing usually involves petrochemicals and in part because these oils are devoid of flavor. Canola is from a variety of rapeseed that has been modified to lower its amount of erucic acid, a substance that may have adverse effects on human health. Grapeseed oil is a by-product of the wine industry, and if there were a more environmentally gentle method of production, it could be a decent option for a neutral-tasting oil. But currently there isn't, so it's not.

PEPPERCORNS: Whole black peppercorns are vastly superior to pre-ground pepper for a simple reason: Once the outer black mantle of a peppercorn is cracked, its volatile oils begin to dissipate. For the best pepper flavor, always begin with whole peppercorns. The same is true for white peppercorns; cracking or grinding them at the last minute ensures the most flavor. Penzeys Spices is an excellent mail-order source (see Resources, page 174). Penzeys also has good dried green peppercorns. Reese brand brined green peppercorns, available in almost any supermarket, are excellent. So-called pink peppercorns are not peppercorns (they come from a type of rose shrub), and their flavor is not pepper-like in any way. I do not recommend them.

SALT: Salt has two essential functions when it comes to salad dressings. First, as it does with all foods, salt facilitates the full blossoming of flavors in dressings. It also balances acid, which can be very helpful if you find yourself faced with an overly acidic dressing.

Today, there are dozens of salts on the shelves of high-end markets, with claims that can make your head spin. Is one really better than another? And how many types of salt do you need?

I recommend three salts. First, you should have Diamond Crystal kosher salt, the default salt in most professional kitchens for good reason. The individual flakes are very dry and very soft, which means they dissolve quickly on the palate, delivering flavors at the same time. This salt is easy to grab with your fingers, and it is inexpensive. You won't find a better all-purpose salt.

Maldon sea salt is similar to Diamond Crystal kosher salt, but the flakes are substantially larger. It is also fairly expensive, making it impractical as an all-purpose salt. Yet the dry flakes tickle your palate like tiny jewels for your tongue to savor. Use it as a finishing salt, sprinkled on a dish immediately before serving.

For a third salt, I recommend *sel gris*, the gray salt from Brittany; *fleur de sel*, a more delicate salt from those same salt pans of northwest France; or the beautiful Hawaiian *alaea* salt, pale orange from natural clay dissolved in the brine. These salts should be used for finishing a dish, not for general cooking, as their unique qualities disappear the moment they dissolve in liquid.

I probably have 30 or 40 salts in my pantry, but in this instance it is best to do as I say, not as I do. When it comes to salt, I'm a nut case, as evidenced by my book *Salt & Pepper* (Broadway, 1999).

SPICES: It's a good idea to buy spices in quantities that you'll use within a year. In most instances, you should replace older spices if you want optimum flavor. Whole spices—whole cloves, allspice berries, cardamom pods, star anise, and so forth—have a longer shelf life, but it is nonetheless a good idea to give your spice cabinet a good cleaning once a year. Penzeys Spices (see Resources, page 174) is an excellent resource, but be sure to check a farmers' market near you, as small purveyors are increasingly common.

SUGAR: Sugar is essential, and not just for the sweetness it contributes. With certain types of salad dressings, a bit of sugar will boost flavors in unexpected ways. For example, a pinch in a raspberry or other fruit vinaigrette will increase our palate's perception of the fruit without actually making the dressing taste sweet. Novice cooks tend to add more vinegar to intensify flavors, but this is futile and only increases acidity, throwing proportions out of balance. Sugar also helps keep the palate open. Professional vinegar tasters use sugar cubes soaked in the vinegar to judge its flavor; they hold the cube to their lips, suck out the vinegar, and discard the sugar cube. The sugar tricks the taste buds into remaining open, so that the taster can evaluate the nuances of flavor; without it, the palate quickly shuts down in the presence of acetic acid.

VINEGAR: The production of artisan vinegars, many of the best from California wine country, has exploded in the past decade. Some of these vinegars are available nationwide—O's very fine vinegars, for example, and those from B.R. Cohn—but most are available only locally, often at farmers' markets.

A well-stocked pantry should have, at a minimum, five vinegars: a white wine or champagne vinegar, a red wine vinegar, a Spanish sherry vinegar, a rice wine vinegar, and a good-quality balsamic vinegar. You may want a raspberry vinegar, too. For white wine vinegar, I recommend Banyuls vinegar, an aged vinegar from the south of France; you'll find it in 500-milliliter bottles labeled "Banyuls Wine Vinegar." It's a bit pricey, though, so you'll probably want a less expensive white wine vinegar as well. For red wine vinegars, there are countless good ones. Look for those with acid no higher than 6 percent. I prefer those made from a single grape varietal, especially Cabernet Sauvignon, as I like their richness, complexity, and depth of flavor.

Finding a good balsamic vinegar is trickier. First, a true *aceto balsamico tradizionale* should never be used in a prepared dish of any kind. These vinegars cost up to hundreds of dollars for a few ounces and should be applied sparingly—with an eyedropper!—to distribute small amounts over a finished dish. Inexpensive commercial balsamic vinegars vary widely in quality. The most important thing is to read the ingredients list and select a vinegar without additions such as sugar, caramel, and vanilla, all of which are added in an attempt to mimic the taste of the real thing but which fall quite short. I use DaVero True Balsamic Vinegar (see Resources, page 173) and find the brand's champagne vinegar, red wine vinegar, and estate olive oil outstanding, too.

WELL-STOCKED COUNTERS AND CUPBOARDS

Even the tiniest kitchen can contain all that is necessary to cook well. And when it comes to salad dressings, you don't need much: just a few bowls, a Mason jar or two, and a few good tools.

A **large wooden cutting board** is essential. "Wood?" you say. "Really?" Yes, really. Although commercial food businesses were first encouraged and then forced to switch from wood to plastic in the 1980s, more recent studies confirm what many of us understood intuitively: that food-grade hardwood is better. Test after test confirms that wood has natural antibacterial qualities. Plastic, on the other hand, has one thing going for it: You can put it in a dishwasher. Yet even after it has gone through the cycle, a plastic cutting board has a high bacteria count, so that's not much of a benefit, is it?

Wood also is kinder to knives; plastic will dull a knife fairly quickly. Wood will eventually wear down a knife's edge, but nowhere near as rapidly as plastic will. If you invest in good knives, invest in a good wooden cutting board, too. If you cook a lot, it helps to have at least two boards—one for meat, fish, and seafood, and one for fruits and vegetables. I have three large ones and too many small ones to count.

A high-quality knife is essential, too, and you really should have two, a **non-serrated paring knife** and an **all-purpose chef's knife**. Add specialized knives as you find you need and can afford them. The best place to get good knives is at a specialty store, where you should try several brands to find one that best fits your hand. Among the better brands, blades are comparable, but handles vary a great deal. It is essential to choose a knife that you can hold for as long as necessary without your hand cramping or growing tired. When a knife is a comfortable fit, cooking is much more enjoyable. And this is one area where thrift is not wise. Cheap knives perform poorly and need to be replaced frequently; a high-quality knife should last a lifetime.

I believe that every kitchen should have a large **suribachi**, or Japanese mortar and pestle. It consists of a wooden pestle and a porcelain bowl that is scored on the inside, which facilitates grinding and crushing. With a suribachi, in just minutes it is easy to reduce a handful of peeled garlic cloves to a smooth paste that is impossible to achieve in a food processor. You can also use it to crush peppercorns and other spices and to pound herbs into a paste. You can put the bowl of a suribachi into a dishwasher and, perhaps best of all, it is an inexpensive item, costing between $10 and $30 depending on size and where you purchase it. The best source is an Asian market.

Your kitchen should be stocked with both a **standard whisk** and a bulb-shaped **balloon whisk**. A sturdy balloon whisk incorporates air quickly and is the best tool for making stable emulsions, like mayonnaise and aioli. When you have both a suribachi and a balloon whisk, you can make such sauces directly in the porcelain bowl and serve them in the bowl, too, as a suribachi is beautiful as well as useful.

These are, in my opinion, the most important items to have in your kitchen. Of course, it goes without saying that all kitchens should have a liquid measuring cup, a set of dry measuring cups, a set of measuring spoons, and good, sturdy wooden spoons, the kind with thick rather than spindly handles. It's also helpful to have a lot of small and medium glass bowls and several large stainless-steel bowls.

For making salad dressings, I like having plenty of wide-mouthed canning jars around, too, for both preparation and storage. I use half-pint jars most often but also keep pint and quart jars in the cupboard for times when I need to make larger quantities.

A food processor or blender has its place, though it is not as essential as we have come to believe. A food processor is most useful when you need to make a stable emulsion in hot weather. I used to make as much as eight gallons of aioli from scratch for a special event I hosted every summer for several years, and most of the time, I did so by hand in small batches. But one year it was blisteringly hot, and I could not get a stable emulsion going in my suribachi. I switched to a food processor and all was fine.

Of all the types and brands I've used over the years, the KitchenAid food processor I purchased recently is my favorite. Because it has a small work bowl and blade that fit within the standard-size work bowl, it can be used for both small and large quantities.

HOW TO HOLD A KNIFE
AND OTHER ESSENTIAL SKILLS

If you can pour, squeeze, and hold a fork, you can make great salad dressings. No special skills or techniques are required and none enhance the process, which is simple and straightforward. However, there are certain general skills that will make your life in the kitchen much easier, and it is pretty simple to master them.

Everyone should learn how to hold a knife properly, with all four fingers and the thumb curled around a comfortable handle. Don't use your pointer finger to steady the blade. It's a bad habit and a dangerous one, should the knife tip over or slip. Keep the fingers of your other hand curled under, and move the ingredients you are cutting, not your hand.

It is also important to know how to keep your knives properly sharpened; dull knives cause more injuries than sharp ones because they don't function properly. If you can't master sharpening knives yourself, get them professionally sharpened once a year. Your local knife shop should offer the service, and increasingly, mobile knife sharpeners are setting up at farmers' markets, where they will take care of your knives (and other blades, such as scissors and pruning shears) while you shop.

Knowing how to select the right tools for specific tasks, while not exactly a technique, is important, too. For example, amateur cooks tend to choose the smallest implement possible for whatever they are doing—the smallest bowl, the smallest saucepan, even the smallest cutting board. Although this might intuitively seem correct, it is not always the best way to go, as experience will show. When it comes to mixing salad dressing and tossing salads, you want space beyond the minimum required to hold the ingredients. In most instances, you should choose a vessel a bit larger than you think you'll need, until you get the hang of it. Eventually, you'll know automatically what size container works best for any cooking activity.

Use a flexible rubber spatula and not a knife or spoon to scrape the sides of bowls, and use a wooden spoon for tasting hot foods, including warm vinaigrettes.

Finally, the proper use of salt is an essential but often overlooked skill. The best cooks and chefs understand that it is essential to add salt as you cook, in stages. In a salad dressing, salt is often added to garlic, shallots, and acid and then added again a time or two before the dish is complete. This allows each ingredient or group of ingredients to blossom fully before the next ingredients are added. Novices think this means adding more salt than usual, but salting in stages usually results in using less salt overall. Pasta is a perfect example. If you cook pasta in unsalted water, no amount of salt added to the finished dish will bring it to full flavor.

For this reason, I call for only "kosher salt" in most recipes, without specifying a quantity. I don't want you to measure. Instead, keep a salt box, salt pig, or other container with a large opening near your main cooking stations. When instructed to season with salt, add a few pinches. At the end of the recipe, when you're ready to correct for salt, taste first, add a few pinches of salt as needed, taste again, and repeat as necessary until flavors are fully blossomed and integrated. Before long, you'll get the hang of it and wonder why you ever bothered to measure salt.

FOOD SAFETY: IT'S ALL ABOUT COMMON SENSE

I use raw eggs. I've used them since I was eight years old and taught myself how to make traditional Caesar salad. I use them in mayonnaise, aioli, similar emulsified sauces, and Caesar salad made directly in the bowl.

I also prefer meat rare and oysters raw.

Life is full of risks, and these are ones I choose to take.

But I've never had a problem, in part because of how I shop. For the most part, the meat, poultry, fish, and shellfish that I buy come from local ranches and the nearby coast. Fruits and vegetables have been sources, nationally, of severe food poisoning in recent years, but I purchase these exclusively from small local farms.

The eggs I use come from three sources. Friends and neighbors share the eggs their backyard hens lay, and these days, I often need no others, as keeping chickens is increasingly popular. I have been well supplied with these eggs for the past several years.

If I do need more eggs, I get them from the little egg stands on the back roads of Sonoma County, where I live, or from a local farmers' market. In all cases, I know how the chickens live and what they eat. Sometimes I even know their names. They are all pastured, which means they run around doing the things chickens like to do, from scratching the ground for grubs and enforcing their pecking orders to taking frequent dirt baths, which helps keep them free of mites.

Eggs from these happy chickens taste better than their supermarket equivalents, and have more nutrients and less chance of contamination. Unlike supermarket eggs, these eggs are typically not washed, which means the natural protective layer that seals the egg remains intact. Simply wash these eggs immediately before using them.

Other safety matters are primarily common sense. Don't leave proteins, including foods with raw eggs, at room temperature for too long. Don't cross-contaminate foods (letting liquid from, say, raw chicken drip onto lettuce). Wash your cutting boards and knives frequently and your hands more frequently. Clean up as you go.

A word about olive oil is in order, too, as adding ingredients to olive oil to flavor it remains quite popular. It's not a good idea. Garlic, for example, can carry invisible spores of *Clostridium botulinum*, which flourishes in anaerobic (oxygen-free) environments, such as olive oil, and can cause botulism. There's no good reason to flavor olive oils, anyway; additional flavors are best added at the last minute, when their flavors will be bright, fresh, and uncompromised by preservatives. Remember, the fresher, the better; that's always the way to go.

WHY THESE RECIPES AND NOT OTHERS?

When choosing which recipes to include in this book, I considered several factors. First, always, is taste: Any recipe must be absolutely delicious to make its way into one of my books. Each of the recipes here is versatile, too, which is to say suitable for a range of salads, not just a single esoteric dish. Ease of preparation and accessibility of ingredients play a role as well; my style of cooking is active and inclusive, a participatory activity and not a spectator sport. If you find yourself with this book in your hands, I hope you will cook from it. That said, these recipes are not set in stone. Each is simply one way to get to a destination. Make the recipes your own, with adjustments, changes, additions, and deletions that reflect not just your preferences but also the environment—the landscape, the climate—in which you live.

I have acknowledged some of the world's classic salad dressings here, too, in part because they are good, we like them, and homemade versions are better than their commercial counterparts, and in part because context and history are important. One can't make a vinaigrette without standing on the shoulders of the world's first vinaigrette, and one shouldn't talk about creamy salad dressings without acknowledging ranch dressing, long the most popular dressing in the United States.

I have assigned each dressing a selection of adjectives that describe its primary characteristics and flavor profile. These terms are meant to serve as guides to assist you in choosing exactly what you want at any given time. If you are looking for an entirely savory dressing, for example, you don't want to be surprised by one with a sweet flourish. The terms are self-explanatory, but let me add a bit of clarification anyway:

• **Savory** means, simply, not sweet; **sweet** implies that sweetness is a dominant characteristic.

• **Warm** addresses the temperature of the dressing, while **cool** indicates that there is an essential refreshing quality.

• **Spicy** heralds the presence of spice—think caraway, for example, or cinnamon—and **hot** announces the heat of chiles and peppers.

• **Creamy** indicates the presence of ingredients that cushion the palate and fill the mouth voluptuously, while **rich** indicates a depth of flavor—think of anchovies—that is sometimes described as umami, or the fifth taste.

• **Tangy** and **tart** both indicate bright acidity; tangy is more gentle and tart makes you pucker a bit. Think of the difference between low-acid vinegar and high-acid vinegar or between certain types of citrus, all of which are somewhat tangy but only some of which can accurately be described as tart.

• **Fragrant** announces that the aromatic quality of a dish—its bouquet, we could say—is an essential quality of the dressing's character, something more than the aromas all foods have.

Following each recipe is a "Best Uses" note, describing those dishes that work best with a particular dressing. The purpose of these recommendations is twofold. First, I want to let you know the best *salads* for the dressings. Second, I hope to expand how you think of dressings by suggesting uses beyond salads, and these notes seem the most efficient way to accomplish this goal.

The majority of the dressing recipes yield small quantities. I use this approach because the dressings are so easy to prepare and because they are at their peak of flavor when first made. There really is no benefit to making more than you can use quickly. A few recipes do make larger quantities, either because they are best suited for dishes that call for more dressing or because the ingredients don't realistically lend themselves to small amounts.

When I must store a vinaigrette or other dressing, I prefer wide-mouthed Mason, Kerr, Ball, Weck, or other canning jars. These jars are durable, stackable, easy to clean, and attractive in a humble way. You do not need cruets or other pretty containers for these recipes; save them for when you're hosting a party. When you need to set the dressing on the table, attractive cruets and bottles are just the thing.

Finally, the book's last chapter, "Sassy and Spirited Salads to Enjoy All Year," cannot, at just 13 recipes, be considered comprehensive. Think of it as a survey, like those intro classes—"Survey of World Literature" and such—from college. In this chapter, I gather my favorite salads, the ones I enjoy day after day, week after week, and month after month, and offer not just a template recipe for each but also seasonal and other variations.

CHAPTER 1

Call It
Vinaigrette

Insalata, the Italian word for salad, simply means "that which is salted."

At its simplest, a vinaigrette is made in a big wooden bowl moments before a salad is served. Here's how it works: Fill the bowl with a generous handful of very good, very fresh greens for each person, sprinkle them with Diamond Crystal kosher salt or Maldon sea salt, and toss them a bit. Drizzle with a little olive oil, add a very small splash of good vinegar or a light squeeze of citrus juice, and toss again.

That's it.

Freshly ground pepper is optional.

If this sounds dull, you've probably been eating too much bottled dressing. Variations on this simple and delightful template are infinite, or nearly so. With so few ingredients, you can vary the flavor tremendously simply by changing the oil or acid. Use a soft late-harvest olive oil, for example, or toasted peanut oil paired with rice wine vinegar. If you want more zing than simple lettuces provide, don't load on a heavy commercial dressing; instead, add a generous handful of fresh herbs—mint, basil, cilantro, thyme, oregano, chervil, or tarragon—with the leaves torn into pieces if they are big. For a burst of garlic, rub the inside of the bowl with a cut clove before adding the greens. Need cheese? Add a handful of crumbled feta or blue cheese. The hallmark of our daily salad is simplicity, and once you've gotten into the habit you'll not want to be without it.

For salads other than simple leafy greens and for the myriad other foods that welcome a vinaigrette, you'll want to make the dressing in a small bowl or jar. Still, it shouldn't take more than a few minutes to do so.

Today vinaigrette is one of the most important flavor-makers around. You'll find it used not only tossed with salad greens but also as a sauce for meats, fish, vegetables, and even desserts.

—Chef John Ash, *Cooking One on One: Private Lessons in Simple, Contemporary Food from a Master Teacher* (Clarkson Potter, 2004)

WHITE WINE VINAIGRETTE

SAVORY

TANGY

TART

FRAGRANT

Here is one of the world's classic salad dressings, welcome on almost any kind of green salad and on a host of other dishes as well. Because there are so few ingredients, their quality determines the success or failure of the dressing; it is essential to use the best ingredients available. Use the smaller amount of olive oil if you prefer a boldly tart vinaigrette; for a milder vinaigrette, use the full 4 tablespoons. For the lemon juice, let the flavor of the vinegar guide you. Some white wine vinegars are suave and complex, while others have either an unpleasant sharpness or what I call "holes," gaps in flavor that lemon juice will usually fill; lemon juice will also smooth the sharpness in most instances.

MAKES ABOUT ⅓ CUP

1 small shallot, minced
1 tablespoon best-quality white wine vinegar, such as Banyuls
1 teaspoon freshly squeezed lemon juice, or as needed
Kosher salt
3 to 4 tablespoons extra-virgin olive oil
Black pepper in a mill

Put the shallot in a small bowl, add the vinegar and lemon juice, and season with salt. Let sit for 15 to 20 minutes.

Use a fork to mix in the olive oil. Season with several turns of black pepper. Taste, and correct for salt and pepper as needed. Use immediately.

Variations

GARLIC VINAIGRETTE: Add 2 minced garlic cloves with the shallots.

PARSLEY VINAIGRETTE: Add 1 tablespoon minced fresh Italian parsley after adding the olive oil.

SIMPLE MUSTARD VINAIGRETTE: Stir 2 teaspoons Dijon mustard into the shallot-and-vinegar mixture before adding salt.

CAPER VINAIGRETTE: Rinse 1 tablespoon capers, chop them, and add along with the shallots.

SPICED VINAIGRETTE: Add about 1 teaspoon of an individual spice or herb. The best choices with this vinaigrette are ground coriander, cardamom, celery seeds, chervil, fennel seeds or pollen, and mustard seeds; good herbs to use are fresh chervil and tarragon, chopped.

RASPBERRY VINAIGRETTE: Replace the white wine vinegar with raspberry vinegar, preferably low acid (5 to 6 percent, no higher) and add a pinch of sugar along with the salt. If the raspberry flavor is too mild, add another pinch of sugar, not to make it sweet but to heighten the raspberry flavors.

BEST USES

Green salad; sliced tomato salad; sliced cucumbers; onion salad; jasmine rice salad; grilled peach and burrata salad; sautéed fish; grilled shrimp with parsley; warm potato salad

SAVORY

TANGY

RICH

Classic red wine vinaigrette is nearly as ubiquitous as white wine vinaigrette and in some parts of the world is the most common way to dress a salad. It is best with a really good red wine vinegar, with low to moderate acidity—no higher than 6 percent, or 60 grain—and a rich flavor. Vinegars made from specific wine varietals are often the best.

MAKES ABOUT ⅔ CUP

1 small shallot, minced, or 1 tablespoon minced red onion
2 tablespoons best-quality red wine vinegar
Kosher salt
6 to 8 tablespoons extra-virgin olive oil
Black pepper in a mill

Put the shallot in a medium bowl, add the vinegar, season with salt, and let sit for 15 to 20 minutes.

Use a fork to stir in the olive oil. Taste, correct for salt as needed, and season with several turns of black pepper. Use immediately, or store, covered, at cool room temperature for up to 3 days.

Variations

ITALIAN HERB VINAIGRETTE: Add 1 or 2 minced garlic cloves and either 2 teaspoons dried Italian herbs or 2 tablespoons minced fresh Italian herbs (mixed Italian parsley, oregano, marjoram, and rosemary).

RICHER RUBY VINAIGRETTE: To either the simple vinaigrette or the one with Italian herbs, add 1 minced garlic clove and either 1 teaspoon anchovy paste or 2 mashed anchovies, along with a bit—about 1 teaspoon—of fresh lemon juice.

RICHER VEGETARIAN RUBY VINAIGRETTE: Mash 2 cloves roasted garlic into a smooth puree and whisk it into the vinegar and shallots.

SPICED RUBY VINAIGRETTE: Add about 1 teaspoon of an individual spice or herb. The best choices with red wine vinegar are ground allspice, cinnamon, cloves, juniper berries, and star anise.

BEST USES

Green salad; green salad with fresh herbs; bread salad; bread and sausage salad; fried caciocavallo cheese with arugula and grilled bread; roasted peppers and tomatoes, with or without sliced mozzarella; chopped salad with Gorgonzola; grilled sardines with frisée and roasted peppers

SAVORY

TANGY

CREAMY

Eggs—poached, soft-boiled, hard-boiled, grated—make wonderful additions to salads, especially when you add a lively vinaigrette. This classic creamy vinaigrette, which relies on a raw egg yolk for its voluptuous character, echoes the richness of poached and soft-boiled eggs and adds a refreshing sparkle that gathers everything into delicious harmony, making it an ideal dressing for salads that feature cooked eggs.

MAKES ABOUT ⅔ CUP

1 shallot, minced
1 garlic clove, minced
1 egg yolk
2 tablespoons heavy cream
Kosher salt
Black pepper in a mill
6 tablespoons mild olive oil or peanut oil
2 tablespoons best-quality white wine vinegar, such as Banyuls, or
    freshly squeezed lemon juice

Put the shallot, garlic, egg yolk, and cream in a small bowl and whisk vigorously for about 1 ½ minutes.

Season with salt and several turns of pepper and whisk again. Slowly whisk in the oil. When the oil is fully incorporated, whisk in the vinegar. Taste, and correct for salt and pepper as needed. Use immediately, or refrigerate, covered, for up to 2 days.

Variation

RED VELVET VINAIGRETTE: Use a rich red wine vinegar, such as B. R. Cohn Cabernet Sauvignon Vinegar or O Zinfandel Vinegar, in place of the white wine or lemon juice. This vinaigrette is excellent with a chopped parsley and caper salad served alongside roasted marrowbones.

BEST USES

Soft-cooked eggs over spring greens; slow-cooked eggs with julienned celery root and crab; poached eggs with roasted asparagus; poached leeks with egg mimosa; grilled salmon salad; cherry tomato, potato, and hard-cooked-egg salad; salad Niçoise; grilled tuna salad; chopped salad

BALSAMIC VINAIGRETTE

SAVORY

SWEET

TANGY

RICH

CREAMY

The simplest balsamic vinaigrette requires nothing more than good vinegar, good olive oil, a bit of salt, and a few turns of black pepper; it's a perfect daily salad dressing, if your preferences lean toward this popular vinegar. This version is richer than that simple mixture, with a layering of flavors that is quite compelling, especially when made with excellent ingredients.

MAKES ABOUT ¾ CUP

1 shallot, minced

1 garlic clove, minced

1 oil-packed anchovy, drained and mashed

Kosher salt

3 tablespoons balsamic vinegar

2 teaspoons honey, warmed, or 2 teaspoons sugar

2 teaspoons Dijon mustard

Black pepper in a mill

1 tablespoon minced fresh herbs (any combination of Italian parsley,
    chives, oregano, thyme, marjoram, and/or rosemary)

½ cup plus 1 tablespoon extra-virgin olive oil

Put the shallot, garlic, and anchovy in a small bowl, season with salt, and stir in the vinegar. Let sit for 15 to 20 minutes.

Add the honey and Dijon mustard and mix well. Season with several turns of black pepper, add the herbs, and then add the olive oil and whisk thoroughly. Taste, and correct for salt, pepper, sweetness, and acid as needed. Use immediately, or refrigerate, covered, for up to 3 days.

RECIPE CONTINUES

Variations

CREAMY BALSAMIC VINAIGRETTE: Add 2 tablespoons crème fraîche.

FRAGRANT BALSAMIC VINAIGRETTE: Add 1 teaspoon pure vanilla extract and extra black pepper. This is delicious with poached lobster salad; roasted quail, chicken, or duck; and any smoked poultry salad.

LAVENDER VINAIGRETTE: At least half an hour before preparing the dressing, put 1 tablespoon culinary-grade lavender flowers in a small bowl, pour the balsamic vinegar over them, and let sit for 30 to 60 minutes. Strain the vinegar and discard the lavender before proceeding.

BEST USES

Mozzarella salad; sliced tomato and mozzarella salad; bread and sausage salad; grilled or roasted root vegetables; grilled portobello mushrooms; roasted beet salad; salads with roasted or smoked poultry; grilled apricots filled with ricotta; grilled peach salad; grilled fig salad; frittatas, especially asparagus and spring onion frittata

NOT YO' MAMA'S
ROASTED GARLIC VINAIGRETTE

SAVORY

FRAGRANT

Most roasted garlic salad dressings are creamy, rich, and heavy. This one is just the opposite. It is light, ethereal even, and has barely enough vinegar to qualify as a vinaigrette. Yet it gains a deeply satisfying flavor from the liquid in which the garlic has been roasted, the secret to its success.

MAKES ABOUT ⅔ CUP

1 firm garlic bulb, loose skins removed, root end cleaned of dirt
   and grit
2 or 3 sprigs thyme
2 to 3 tablespoons water
6 tablespoons extra-virgin olive oil
Kosher salt
Black pepper in a mill
1 tablespoon best-quality white wine vinegar, such as Banyuls,
   plus more to taste
1 teaspoon fresh thyme leaves
2 teaspoons snipped fresh chives

Preheat the oven to 350°F.

Put the garlic bulb, root end down, in a small ovenproof container, add the thyme sprigs and water, and pour the oil over the garlic. Season with salt and pepper, cover, and roast until the garlic is as tender as soft butter, anywhere from 40 to 60 minutes. To test, press the fattest part of a clove with your thumb.

When the garlic is fully tender, remove it from the oven, uncover, and let cool. Transfer the roasted garlic to a container and reserve for another use. Strain the cooking liquid into a small bowl or small wide-mouthed Mason jar. Add the vinegar, thyme leaves,

RECIPE CONTINUES

and chives, taste, and correct for salt, pepper, and acid as needed. Use immediately, or refrigerate, covered, for up to 5 days.

Variation

CREAMY ROASTED GARLIC VINAIGRETTE: Mash 2 of the roasted garlic cloves until very smooth, add to the vinaigrette, and stir or shake to combine. For an even creamier version, add 1 tablespoon crème fraîche along with the mashed roasted garlic, and mix thoroughly.

BEST USES

Simple green salad; salad of greens and fresh herbs; thinly sliced celery; sliced tomato salad; corn salad; arugula and red onion salad; arugula with Parmigiano-Reggiano curls; roasted chicken salad; frittata with leeks and spring garlic

CREAMY LEMON CITRONETTE

Lemon vinaigrette: We see it all the time and it is arguably one of the most popular salad dressings, right up there with balsamic vinaigrette and white wine vinaigrette. Yet, technically, it's not a vinaigrette but rather a citronette, and I'm calling it such in honor of the grammarians of the world, who follow along sweeping up the debris of our ever-evolving, or devolving, language. But most often, I too call it vinaigrette.

I usually make lemon citronette in the salad bowl itself, right before serving it, and use only salt, fresh lemon juice, olive oil, and black pepper. If I want other flavors—blue cheese, say, or sliced red onion—they go into the bowl with the lettuce. But there are times when I want more layers of flavor and texture in my lemon dressing, as when I am making grain, bean, or seafood salads.

MAKES ABOUT ⅔ CUP

1 small shallot, minced
1 or 2 garlic cloves, minced
1 teaspoon grated lemon zest
2 tablespoons freshly squeezed lemon juice
Kosher salt
6 tablespoons extra-virgin olive oil
1 tablespoon crème fraîche
1 tablespoon snipped fresh chives
Black pepper in a mill

Put the shallot, garlic, and lemon zest in a mixing bowl or small wide-mouthed Mason jar, add the lemon juice, and let sit for 15 to 20 minutes.

Season generously with salt, add the olive oil, and either mix with a fork or small whisk or seal the jar and shake it vigorously. Add the crème fraîche and mix or shake again. RECIPE CONTINUES

Add the chives, season generously with black pepper, taste, and correct for salt as needed. The dressing is best served immediately but may be refrigerated for up to 2 days.

Variations

LEMON CITRONETTE: Simply omit the crème fraîche.

LIME CITRONETTE: Replace the lemon zest and juice with lime zest and juice and the chives with cilantro.

PRESERVED LEMON CITRONETTE: Replace the lemon zest with 1 tablespoon minced preserved lemon peel.

BEST USES

Butter lettuce; butter lettuce with thinly sliced red onion and crumbled blue cheese; chickpea, celery, and tuna salad; pasta salad; sautéed fish; roasted chicken salad; Sicilian-style shellfish salad; Greek-style salad; farro salad; rice and bean salads

LIME-CAYENNE CITRONETTE

SAVORY

TART

HOT

The slow burn, which builds as this vinaigrette lingers on the palate, is absolutely addictive, in a good way. This is my dressing of choice for scallop ceviche, which I make by marinating little bay scallops in fresh lime juice and salt for 3 to 4 hours. I drain the marinated scallops thoroughly, add a good bit of minced red onion and this dressing, and then serve the ceviche over butter lettuce; I sometimes top it with avocado drizzled with a bit of the vinaigrette. If you love cilantro, add a shower of chopped leaves.

MAKES ABOUT ½ CUP

¼ cup freshly squeezed lime juice
1 serrano chile, seeded and minced
3 garlic cloves, minced
Kosher salt
⅛ to ¼ teaspoon ground cayenne pepper, to taste
Black pepper in a mill
⅓ cup extra-virgin olive oil

Put the lime juice in a small bowl, add the serrano and garlic, season with salt, and stir in the cayenne. Add several turns of black pepper and whisk in the olive oil. Taste, and correct for salt as needed. Use immediately.

BEST USES

Scallop ceviche; halibut or scallop carpaccio on microgreens; halibut gravlax; seafood and shellfish salad; quinoa and corn salad

CARAWAY VINAIGRETTE

This dressing illustrates beautifully how two salad dressings often make the best salad. When I make Russian Egg Potato Salad (page 150), I marinate the warm potatoes in this dressing before adding onions, blanched diced carrots, English peas, mustard, and mayonnaise. The salad is then topped with deviled eggs that are themselves crowned with a dollop of caviar. The presentation is spectacular, as is the taste. Without this vinaigrette, the salad would be good but unremarkable.

Caraway itself is interesting, not only as a spice but also as a plant. It is a member of the Umbelliferae family, which includes carrots, celery, hemlock, parsley, and parsnips. What we call the seeds are actually the caraway plant's fruit. The roots, like the roots of parsley, can be prepared similarly to carrots and parsnips. Should you have some, try them roasted and drizzled with this vinaigrette.

MAKES ABOUT ¾ CUP

1 small shallot, minced

2 garlic cloves, minced

¾ teaspoon caraway seeds, toasted and crushed

2 tablespoons red wine vinegar

Juice of 1 lemon

2 teaspoons minced fresh Italian parsley

1 teaspoon minced fresh oregano

1 teaspoon minced fresh thyme

1 teaspoon celery seeds

Kosher salt

Black pepper in a mill

½ cup extra-virgin olive oil

In a small bowl, mix together the shallot, garlic, and caraway seeds. Pour the vinegar and lemon juice over the mixture and let sit for 15 to 20 minutes.

Mix in the parsley, oregano, thyme, and celery seeds. Season with salt and several turns of black pepper and whisk in the olive oil. Taste, and correct for salt, pepper, oil, and acid as needed. Use immediately, or refrigerate, covered, for up to 2 days.

BEST USES

Warm potato salad; Russian Egg Potato Salad; roasted beets over fresh greens; shredded cabbage; steamed carrots; grilled cheese sandwich made with rye bread and cheddar

Unrefined walnut oil is delicious, fragile, and expensive. Store it in the refrigerator and use it within 3 months. You can, if you prefer, use all walnut oil in this dressing, though I find that diluting it with another oil results in a more balanced vinaigrette.

MAKES ABOUT 1 CUP

1 shallot, minced
2 tablespoons sherry vinegar
2 tablespoons dry red wine
Kosher salt
Black pepper in a mill
2 tablespoons toasted and minced walnuts
2 tablespoons minced fresh Italian parsley
⅓ cup unrefined walnut oil
⅓ cup mild olive oil or peanut oil

Put the shallot, vinegar, and wine in a small bowl, season with salt, and let sit for 15 to 20 minutes.

Season with several generous turns of black pepper and stir in the walnuts and parsley. Whisk in both oils, taste, and correct the seasoning as needed. Stir or shake well before using. Use immediately, or refrigerate, covered, for up to 2 days.

BEST USES

Roasted beets; salad of roasted beets, feta cheese, pomegranate arils, and toasted walnuts; wild rice with dried cranberries; grilled scallops over frisée; spaghetti squash salad; sweet potato salad

HAZELNUT VINAIGRETTE

SAVORY

FRAGRANT

Hazelnut oil, like walnut and many other nut oils, is fragile and expensive. Buy it in small quantities, store it in the refrigerator, and use it within a few weeks. I find that one of its best uses is with salads that feature pears, so I like to keep it on hand when good pears are in season.

MAKES ABOUT ¾ CUP

1 small shallot, minced
3 tablespoons pear vinegar or champagne vinegar
Pinch of sugar
Kosher salt
1 teaspoon snipped fresh chives
3 tablespoons hazelnut oil
6 tablespoons peanut oil or mild olive oil
Black pepper in a mill

Put the shallot in a small bowl, add the vinegar and pinch of sugar, and season with salt. Let sit for 10 to 20 minutes.

Add the chives and whisk in both of the oils. Taste, correct for salt as needed, and season with several turns of black pepper. Use immediately, or refrigerate, covered, for up to 2 days.

BEST USES

Sliced avocados; roasted asparagus; roasted chicken salad with pears, avocado, and toasted hazelnuts; salad of poached lobster, pears, and toasted hazelnuts

ZINFANDEL VINAIGRETTE

SAVORY

FRAGRANT

RICH

This is a dressing that guys love, perhaps because it also makes an excellent marinade for meats that will be grilled. Thinking seduction? Just put a tri-tip in a freezer bag, add half this dressing, and refrigerate overnight. The next day, grill the tri-tip rare to medium-rare, slice it, and drizzle the remaining vinaigrette on top. Ahhh, love at first bite.

MAKES ABOUT 1½ CUPS

2 shallots, minced

1 teaspoon dried oregano or 2 teaspoons fresh oregano

1 teaspoon kosher salt, plus more to taste

Generous pinch of ground cloves or ground allspice

3 to 4 tablespoons best-quality red wine vinegar or balsamic vinegar

¾ cup Zinfandel or other robust, fruit-driven red wine

Black pepper in a mill

1 cup extra-virgin olive oil

2 teaspoons sugar, if needed

Put the shallots and oregano in a medium Mason jar, and add the salt, cloves, and vinegar. Let sit for 15 to 20 minutes.

Stir in the wine, season very generously with black pepper, add the olive oil, close the jar tightly, and shake it vigorously. Taste, and correct for salt and pepper as needed. If this correction does not boost the flavors and bring them into balance, add the sugar and shake the dressing again. Use within a few hours.

BEST USES

Grilled fig salad; figs stuffed with chèvre, wrapped in bacon, and grilled or broiled; grilled sliced tri-tip; as a marinade and dressing for beef, lamb, or venison

SUNDAY MORNING MIRACLE: BLOODY MARY VINAIGRETTE

SAVORY

TANGY

FRAGRANT

SPICY

HOT

Spending a leisurely Sunday morning in bed, the *New York Times* spread all over and favorite music on the radio, is one of life's great—and, alas, vanishing—joys. Still, there are weekends now and then when this pleasure can be savored, however briefly, in spite of how busy we all seem to be. If one of these moments occurs in late summer, when tomatoes are heavy on the vine, Bloody Marys might enter the picture, and this ethereal vinaigrette reminiscent of that drink will heighten your pleasure. You can, if you like, omit the vodka and still have a delicious dressing.

MAKES ABOUT ⅔ CUP

½ cup fresh tomato water (see Note)
1 tablespoon freshly squeezed lemon juice, plus more to taste
½ teaspoon celery salt
1 to 2 ounces spicy vodka, such as Hangar One Chipotle, Absolut
  Peppar, or a homemade infusion (optional)
2 to 3 tablespoons robust extra-virgin olive oil
Kosher salt
Black pepper in a mill
Tabasco sauce

Put the tomato water and lemon juice in a small wide-mouthed Mason jar, and add the celery salt, vodka (if using), and olive oil. Stir, and season with salt, several turns of black pepper, and a shake or two of Tabasco.

Taste and correct for salt, pepper, heat, and acid. Cover and chill for at least 30 minutes and as long as 3 hours. Use this dressing the day it is made.

Note: To make ½ cup tomato water, peel 3 large tomatoes by spearing them, one at a time, through their stem ends with the tines of a fork and turning them over a flame to sear their skins. Use your fingers to remove the skins. Cut the peeled tomatoes in half through their equators. Set a medium strainer over a deep bowl and squeeze each tomato half gently to remove the seeds and gel. Stir to release the juice; discard the seeds. Chop the tomatoes into a fine pulp, transfer to the strainer and let drain, stirring now and then, for about 10 minutes, until as much juice as possible has been released. Reserve the pulp—called tomato concassé—for another use, such as Warm Tomato Vinaigrette (page 73).

BEST USES

Fried eggs with crisp bacon; poached eggs over toast or polenta; thinly sliced celery; thinly sliced fennel; sliced tomatoes; sliced tomatoes with burrata or mozzarella; spaghettini with shredded lettuce, julienned mozzarella, and crisp bacon

SAVORY

SWEET

TANGY

At the height of tomato season, farmers' markets are filled with colorful cherry tomatoes that range in size from small grape to Ping-Pong ball. I prefer this dressing made with tomatoes that are roughly the same size—all currant tomatoes, for example. The smallest tomatoes need only to be cut in half; if they're any bigger than currant tomatoes, they should be quartered. If the pieces are too big, this vinaigrette will seem more like a salad.

MAKES 2 ½ TO 3 CUPS

1 shallot, minced

2 garlic cloves, minced

3 tablespoons white wine vinegar or champagne vinegar, plus more
    as needed

2 cups small cherry tomatoes, preferably a mix of orange, yellow,
    and red

Juice of 1 lemon

Kosher salt

Black pepper in a mill

½ cup extra-virgin olive oil, plus more as needed

2 tablespoons minced fresh chives, Italian parsley, basil, or a mixture
    of all three

Put the shallot and garlic in a medium bowl, add the vinegar, and let sit for 15 to 20 minutes.

Meanwhile, cut the cherry tomatoes in half through their equators; if they are particularly large, cut each half in half.

Stir the lemon juice into the shallot mixture and season with salt and several turns of pepper. Stir in the olive oil. Add the herbs, toss gently, taste, and correct for salt,

RECIPE CONTINUES

pepper, oil, and acid as needed. Use within 30 minutes or refrigerate, covered, for up to 2 days. Return to room temperature before serving.

BEST USES

Italian parsley salad (use the vinaigrette sparingly); salad of pasta, corn, and green beans; grilled eggplant; rice salad; simple potato salad; grilled iceberg lettuce wedges; grilled radicchio; grilled cabbage wedges; burrata with arugula; omelets and frittatas

GRAPEFRUIT VINAIGRETTE

SWEET

TANGY

FRAGRANT

The delicacy of freshly squeezed grapefruit juice lends itself to simple, pristine dressings like this one. If you leave out the olive oil, you can drizzle the seasoned juice over oysters on the half shell. And if you can find Sarawak grapefruit, a variety I discovered recently at my local farmers' market, use it! Juice from this pale green grapefruit is so sweet and so delicate that you'll be hooked with your first taste. If you don't have any cardamom seeds, don't worry. I like the way they perfume the grapefruit juice, but the vinaigrette is still delicious without them.

MAKES A SCANT ⅔ CUP

2 tablespoons freshly squeezed grapefruit juice
2 tablespoons champagne vinegar or white wine vinegar
2 or 3 cardamom seeds (optional)
Pinch of sugar
Kosher salt
Black pepper in a mill
6 tablespoons extra-virgin olive oil

Put the grapefruit juice and vinegar in a small bowl, and add the cardamom seeds (if using), sugar, salt, and several turns of black pepper. Stir to dissolve the sugar and salt. Let sit for about 30 minutes so the flavors can meld and blossom. Stir in the olive oil and use immediately.

BEST USES

Leafy greens; avocado and frisée salad; avocado and grapefruit salad; citrus salad; pear salad; chicken salad; crab salad

SAVORY

SWEET

RICH

The first time I visited Sicily, I flew from Milan to Palermo with one of the most interesting flight crews I've ever encountered. Shortly after takeoff, the two male flight attendants pinned up a curtain in the front of the plane, disappeared behind it, and emerged a few minutes later in different uniforms and sporting, somehow, a certain roguish look, enhanced by a day or two's growth of beard and hair that had been disheveled by the quick change. Ahh, Sicily, I thought, you will not disappoint me. Soon they were coming along the aisle with beverages, including tall glasses of ruby-colored blood orange juice, as common there as orange-colored orange juice is here. Although you can make this vinaigrette with any orange, it will lack a certain something—a subtle spicy quality, a visual beauty—if you don't use blood oranges.

MAKES ABOUT ½ CUP

2 tablespoons freshly squeezed blood orange juice
2 tablespoons Cabernet Sauvignon vinegar
Kosher salt
4 to 6 tablespoons extra-virgin olive oil
Black pepper in a mill

Put the orange juice and vinegar in a small bowl, add the salt, and stir a couple of times to dissolve it. Add the olive oil, stir with a fork or whisk, and add several turns of black pepper. Use immediately.

BEST USES
Shredded greens; shredded romaine with thinly sliced fennel and fresh mint leaves; fennel and cucumber salad; Sicilian orange salad with red onion, black olives, and curls of an aged grating cheese

SWEET

TANGY

RICH

Apple cider vinegar is the signature vinegar of America, the first and only vinegar to be legally labeled simply "vinegar." In recent years, many artisan apple cider vinegars have hit the marketplace; they're often available at farmers' markets. These vinegars are usually organic, raw, and unfiltered, which lends a range of flavors not found in most national brands. This vinaigrette is delicious and versatile on its own and at the same time makes a perfect canvas for building other dressings, especially sweet ones (see the Variations).

MAKES A SCANT ⅔ CUP

2 tablespoons apple juice

2 tablespoons apple cider vinegar

¾ teaspoon kosher salt

Black pepper in a mill

6 tablespoons extra-virgin olive oil

Put the apple juice and vinegar in a small bowl, add the salt and several generous turns of black pepper, and stir to dissolve the salt. Mix in the olive oil and use immediately.

Variations

ZESTY APPLE CIDER VINAIGRETTE: Stir in 2 tablespoons apricot, kumquat, or fig jam and 3 or 4 minced garlic cloves. Let sit for at least 15 minutes before serving. This is excellent with roasted pork salads or pork sliders.

MANGO-CIDER VINAIGRETTE: Stir in ½ cup pureed fresh mango, taste, correct for acid and salt, and add 2 tablespoons minced fresh cilantro leaves. This dressing is delicious over sliced pineapple and tropical fruit salads.

RECIPE CONTINUES

SPICY APPLE CIDER VINAIGRETTE: Stir in 2 tablespoons hot pepper jam, taste, and correct for acid and salt. This is best with warm chèvre and leafy greens.

SMOKY APPLE CIDER VINAIGRETTE: Stir in 1 to 2 teaspoons chipotle chile powder, taste, correct for acid and salt, and finish with a tablespoon of crème fraîche. This variation is excellent with a salad of julienned carrots, jicama, and radishes.

BEST USES

Inner leaves of butter lettuce with thinly sliced red onion and crumbled blue cheese; cabbage and apple slaw; grilled quail salad; roasted chicken salad

WATERMELON VINAIGRETTE

SWEET

TANGY

TART

HOT

This dressing illustrates perfectly my approach to both flavors and textures. I prefer pure, pristine flavors and the lean, bright textures that allow such flavors to sparkle on the palate. Most often, I select a single major ingredient and add other ingredients to support it, not eclipse it. Watermelon vinaigrette has become quite popular in the past decade or so; there are even commercial versions. Yet I've never had one that actually tasted like watermelon. Boldly flavored ingredients like red wine vinegar, balsamic vinegar, or honey eclipse the delicate taste of watermelon, as do such additions as cream, sour cream, and crème fraîche. And when it comes to technique, I never, ever put watermelon in a blender or food processor, as it becomes foamy, a quality I find unpleasant and impossible to correct. If you love good watermelon in season—for me, that means late summer and fall—you should love this vinaigrette.

MAKES ABOUT 1¼ CUPS

1 cup fresh watermelon juice (see Note page 57)

1 tablespoon minced red onion

1 teaspoon minced and seeded serrano or jalapeño chile

1 tablespoon freshly squeezed lime juice or best-quality white wine vinegar, such as Banyuls

2 teaspoons simple syrup (see Note page 57)

½ teaspoon kosher salt

2 tablespoons fruity olive oil

1 tablespoon chopped fresh cilantro

Black pepper in a mill

Put the juice in a small bowl or jar, add the onion, chile, lime juice, simple syrup, and salt, and stir. Taste, and correct for salt and acid. Stir in the olive oil, add the cilantro,

RECIPE CONTINUES

and season with several turns of black pepper. Chill for 30 minutes before serving. This vinaigrette is best the day it is made.

Notes: For 1 cup watermelon juice, you'll need about 2¹/₂ cups diced watermelon. Simply cut open a melon, scoop out the flesh, and cut it into small dice. Put the diced watermelon in a strainer set over a deep bowl and stir the watermelon now and then as it drains, 20 to 30 minutes. Occasionally crush the watermelon gently with the side of a spoon, but do not press it through the strainer. Strain the juice before using.

Simple syrup, sold in many stores as bar syrup, is easy to prepare at home. To make it, combine equal quantities of granulated sugar and water in a saucepan set over high heat. Do not stir. Simmer until the sugar is dissolved and the liquid is entirely clear, not cloudy, 5 to 7 minutes. Remove from the heat, let cool, pour into a bottle or jar, and refrigerate. Stored properly, simple syrup keeps almost indefinitely.

BEST USES

Beet carpaccio; halibut carpaccio with microgreens; halibut gravlax; arugula and feta salad; feta and olive salad; salad of julienned jicama, carrots, and radishes; salad of fried haloumi cheese with arugula and toasted pine nuts; fruit salad with whipped ricotta

PERSEPHONE'S PLEASURE: POMEGRANATE VINAIGRETTE

SAVORY

SWEET

TANGY

FRAGRANT

Persephone presides over the island of Sicily, where her signature fruit, the pomegranate, thrives in lush profusion. So does the orange, including the blood orange, which you should use in this recipe if you can find it. For Persephone's sake, use fresh rather than bottled pomegranate juice here; it's quite easy to make.

MAKES ABOUT 1 CUP

1 small shallot, minced
2 tablespoons Banyuls white wine vinegar, champagne vinegar, or
    pomegranate vinegar
Pinch of sugar
Kosher salt
⅓ cup freshly squeezed pomegranate juice (see Note page 60)
Zest of ½ orange, cut into very fine julienne
Black pepper in a mill
⅔ cup mild extra-virgin olive oil

Put the shallot in a small bowl, cover with the vinegar, and let sit for 15 to 20 minutes.

Add the sugar and several generous pinches of salt, and then stir in the pomegranate juice, orange zest, and several turns of black pepper.

Whisk in the olive oil, taste, and correct for salt and pepper as needed. Taste again, and if it's a bit flat, add a pinch more sugar, which will boost the pomegranate flavor. Use immediately, or refrigerate, covered, for up to 2 days.

RECIPE CONTINUES

Note: To make pomegranate juice, begin with a fresh pomegranate. The fastest way to extract the juice is to cut the fruit in half through its equator and ream the halves with a lemon reamer, holding them over a wide bowl, until all of the juice is released. You can also extract the arils and pass them through a food mill fitted with its smallest blade. Strain the juice before using it. A single ripe pomegranate should yield $^1/_3$ to $^1/_2$ cup of juice.

BEST USES

Rice salad with fresh pomegranate arils; wild rice salad, with or without fresh cranberries and pine nuts; rice and bean salads; seared duck breast or smoked duck over fresh greens; salad of butter lettuce, avocado, grapefruit, and pomegranate arils; salad of persimmon, avocado, and seared lamb

CREAMY GREEN PEPPERCORN-MUSTARD VINAIGRETTE

SAVORY

TANGY

SPICY

CREAMY

If you cannot find green peppercorn Dijon mustard, use any good Dijon—Grey Poupon is just fine—and add 1 tablespoon brined green peppercorns, rinsed and crushed lightly.

MAKES ABOUT ¾ CUP

2 garlic cloves, peeled

3 oil-packed anchovy fillets, drained

1 tablespoon freshly squeezed lemon juice, plus more as needed

2 tablespoons green peppercorn Dijon mustard, such as Edmond Fallot brand

2 tablespoons minced fresh Italian parsley

Black pepper in a mill

Kosher salt (optional)

⅔ cup extra-virgin olive oil

Put the garlic in a suribachi (see page 12) or mortar and crush it with a wooden pestle. Add the anchovies and grind with the garlic to form a smooth paste. Stir in the lemon juice, mustard, and parsley and season with several turns of black pepper. Taste, and correct for salt as needed.

Use a whisk to add the olive oil slowly, creating a light emulsion. Use immediately.

BEST USES

Shredded romaine lettuce; salad of roasted chicken, artichokes, and spaghettini (or other similar long thin noodle); cauliflower and broccoli salad; shaved raw Brussels sprouts

GINGER-MUSTARD VINAIGRETTE

SWEET

FRAGRANT

SPICY

HOT

I tend to make coleslaw at least once a week, using whatever vegetables I find at the farmers' market. There's always cabbage and red onion; other options include carrots, fennel, radishes, Brussels sprouts (yes, raw), green onion, celery, jicama, celery root, sunchokes, apples, raspberries, blueberries, and more, depending on the season. I slice everything (except berries) using my KitchenAid food processor's thinnest slicing blade, and I vary the dressings. This one is in regular rotation, and when I use it I add a couple of big handfuls of chopped cilantro.

This dressing is also delicious with pork, especially pork tenderloin. Use it as a marinade when the meat will be oven roasted and then add more after it has been sliced and presented over couscous studded with golden raisins, roasted pistachios, pomegranate arils, and chopped cilantro.

MAKES ABOUT 1 CUP

1 shallot, minced
½ serrano chile, minced (optional)
2 garlic cloves, pressed
2 tablespoons apple cider vinegar or rice wine vinegar
2 tablespoons freshly squeezed lime juice, plus more to taste
1 tablespoon grated fresh ginger
1 tablespoon sugar
Kosher salt
1 tablespoon Dijon mustard
⅔ cup mild extra-virgin olive oil, *or* ⅓ cup roasted peanut oil and
⅓ cup mild olive oil
Black pepper in a mill

Put the shallot in a medium bowl, add the chile (if using), garlic, vinegar, and lime juice, and let sit for a few minutes.

RECIPE CONTINUES

Stir in the ginger and sugar, season with salt, and stir in the mustard. Using a small whisk or a fork, pour in the olive oil, mixing as you do. Add several turns of black pepper.

Taste, and correct for acid and salt as needed. Use within 30 minutes or refrigerate, covered, for up to 2 days.

BEST USES

Vegetable slaw; noodle salad; seafood salad; chicken salad; grilled shrimp over greens; rice, pomegranate, and red onion salad

HONEY VINAIGRETTE

SWEET

TANGY

FRAGRANT

When I want to serve a salad with this dressing following the main meal, as is my preference, I let the shallot macerate in the vinegar while we eat and have everything else at the ready, including already-salted shredded greens in a nearby bowl. It takes just a minute or two to finish making the salad right at the table.

MAKES ABOUT ½ CUP

1 small shallot, minced
3 tablespoons sherry vinegar
Kosher salt
2 teaspoons honey, warmed
Black pepper in a mill
6 tablespoons olive oil

Put the shallot in a small bowl, add the vinegar, season with salt, and let sit for 15 to 20 minutes.

Stir in the warmed honey, add several turns of black pepper, and whisk in the olive oil. Taste, correct for salt as needed, and use immediately.

BEST USES

Shredded greens, with or without feta cheese; as a marinade for thinly sliced sweet onions; wild rice salad; grilled fruit, including apricots, peaches, nectarines, and figs

SWEET

TANGY

FRAGRANT

SPICY

We do not typically think of vinaigrette—or black pepper, for that matter—at dessert time, but this dressing is outrageously great over sliced fresh strawberries, with or without vanilla or black pepper ice cream, or, perhaps surprisingly, with classic New York cheesecake. When selecting vinegar for this dressing, choose a Spanish sherry vinegar for a smooth, suave taste; for something a bit sweeter and more robust, use your favorite balsamic vinegar. This dressing is equally good with pasta, tomatoes, shrimp, and rare lamb.

MAKES ABOUT 1¼ CUPS

1 shallot, minced

4 garlic cloves, minced

1 teaspoon kosher salt, plus more to taste

¼ cup sherry vinegar or balsamic vinegar

1 tablespoon freshly cracked black peppercorns (see Note),
    plus more to taste

¼ cup honey, warmed

⅔ cup extra-virgin olive oil

¼ cup shredded fresh mint (optional)

Put the shallot, garlic, and 1 teaspoon kosher salt in a small bowl, add the vinegar, and let sit for 15 minutes.

Stir in the black pepper, honey, and olive oil. Taste, and correct for salt and pepper as needed. Fold in the mint, if using. The dressing will keep in the refrigerator for up to 2 days but is best the day it is made. If the dressing will be stored in the refrigerator, do not add the mint until ready to serve.

Note: When you crack peppercorns, the pieces are larger than when you grind them. To accomplish this, put the peppercorns in a suribachi (see page 12) and use a wooden pestle to crack each one. You can also crack peppercorns by tucking them into the folds of a clean kitchen towel and rolling over them with a rolling pin. In a pinch, wrap the peppercorns in a towel and crack them with a hammer.

BEST USES

Summer tomato salads, especially cherry tomato salads; pasta salads with baby shrimp and cherry tomatoes; grilled shrimp with or without salad greens; grilled leg of lamb with or without salad greens; rice salads; sliced fresh strawberries

SWEET

TANGY

RICH

I developed this recipe to go specifically with a sweet potato salad I'd been asked to make for a friend's party. I fell in love with it and now use it on everything from simple red onion salads to collard greens cooked with ham hocks.

MAKES ABOUT 2 CUPS

2 tablespoons molasses, warmed

2 tablespoons honey, warmed, plus more as needed

6 tablespoons sherry vinegar, plus more as needed

1 teaspoon kosher salt, plus more to taste

1 small shallot, minced

3 tablespoons toasted chopped pecans (optional)

2 teaspoons freshly ground white pepper

1 cup extra-virgin olive oil, plus more as needed

Put the molasses and honey in a wide-mouthed pint jar, add the vinegar and salt, close the jar tightly, and shake it vigorously until the mixture is smooth. Add the shallot, pecans (if using), white pepper, and olive oil, close the jar, and shake it again.

Taste, and correct for sweetness, acid, salt, and oil as needed. Use immediately, or store, covered, at room temperature for up to 3 days. Shake the dressing vigorously immediately before using.

BEST USES

Salad of sweet potato, red onion, and toasted pecans; salad of spaghetti squash and Spanish chorizo; roasted root vegetable salad; slow-cooked collard greens

SAVORY

SWEET

TANGY

RICH

White miso, the mildest of the fermented soybean and grain pastes, is none-theless intensely flavored and requires equally bold ingredients—here, a significant amount of fresh ginger and seasoned rice vinegar—to make an integrated vinaigrette.

MAKES ABOUT ¾ CUP

¼ cup white miso

2 tablespoons grated fresh ginger

3 garlic cloves, pressed

2 tablespoons seasoned rice wine vinegar

1 tablespoon freshly squeezed lime juice

4 to 5 teaspoons simple syrup (see page 57) or mild honey

1 teaspoon toasted sesame oil

2 tablespoons roasted peanut oil

2 tablespoons hot water, or as needed

Red pepper flakes

2 teaspoons very thinly sliced scallions or chopped fresh cilantro

1 tablespoon toasted white sesame seeds

Put the miso in a small bowl, add the ginger, garlic, vinegar, lime juice, and simple syrup, and whisk. Add both oils and whisk again. Use the hot water to thin to the desired consistency, add the red pepper flakes, and let sit for 15 minutes.

Stir the dressing and add the scallions and sesame seeds. Use immediately, or refrigerate, covered, for up to 5 days.

BEST USES

Shredded cabbage salad; zucchini and carrot ribbons; grilled salmon or shrimp salad; grilled chicken or beef skewers

WARM SHALLOT VINAIGRETTE

SAVORY

WARM

TANGY

You won't find a warm vinaigrette more versatile than this; I consider it as much a classic, as necessary and important, as white wine vinaigrette and lemon citronette. It is important to pay careful attention to the level of heat so that the shallots do not brown or, even worse, burn. Vegetarians can simply omit the pancetta or replace it with about 2 tablespoons minced portobello mushrooms.

MAKES ABOUT 1 CUP

⅔ cup extra-virgin olive oil
2 shallots, minced
3 pancetta slices, diced
2 garlic cloves, minced
Kosher salt
2 tablespoons best-quality white wine vinegar, such as Banyuls
1 tablespoon freshly squeezed lemon juice, plus more to taste
Black pepper in a mill
2 tablespoons minced fresh Italian parsley or snipped fresh chives

Pour a little of the olive oil into a sauté pan set over medium-low heat, add the shallots and pancetta, and sauté gently just until the shallots are soft and fragrant, 7 to 8 minutes. Add the garlic and sauté for 1 1/2 minutes more. Season with salt.

Pour in the vinegar and lemon juice, and simmer for 1 minute. Pour in the remaining olive oil and heat through. Add several turns of black pepper and remove from the heat.

Taste, and correct for salt and acid as needed. (Use lemon juice to adjust acid balance.) Stir in the parsley and use immediately. This dressing is best served the day it is made, but it can be stored, covered, in the refrigerator for up to 2 days, then reheated just before using.

RECIPE CONTINUES

BEST USES

Roasted asparagus; roasted asparagus with poached eggs or egg mimosa; salad of green beans and cherry tomatoes; warm wild mushrooms over triple-cream cheese and leafy greens; feta cheese over frisée, with toasted almonds and grilled grapes; poached leeks, with or without poached eggs; warm green beans, especially Romano-type beans

SAVORY

WARM

TANGY

FRAGRANT

I have a special fondness for this dressing. Although I love it on salads, my favorite way to enjoy it is with olive risotto. After I spoon the creamy risotto into a soup plate, I drizzle some of the vinaigrette both around the risotto and on top of it, so that diners get a little with each bite.

MAKES ABOUT 1 ½ CUPS

1 shallot, minced
2 or 3 garlic cloves, minced
Kosher salt
2 tablespoons best-quality white wine vinegar, such as Banyuls
⅓ cup extra-virgin olive oil, plus more as needed
1 cup tomato concassé (see Note page 74)
Juice of ½ lemon
1 tablespoon minced fresh Italian parsley
1 tablespoon snipped fresh chives
Black pepper in a mill

Put the shallot and garlic in a small bowl, season with salt, and stir in the vinegar. Let sit for 20 minutes.

Pour the olive oil into a small saucepan set over low heat and warm through. Stir in the tomato concassé, lemon juice, and the shallot mixture, and heat, stirring gently, until the mixture is warm; do not let it boil.

Remove from the heat, stir in the parsley and chives, and add several turns of black pepper. Taste, and correct for salt, oil, and acid. Use immediately, or refrigerate, covered, for up to 2 days and then reheat before using.

RECIPE CONTINUES

Note: To make tomato concassé, peel 2 or 3 medium-size backyard-quality tomatoes by spearing them, one at a time, through their stem ends with the tines of a fork and turning them over a hot burner or flame to blister their skins. It takes no more than about 20 seconds per tomato. Use your fingers to peel off the seared skin, then remove the stem core and cut the tomatoes in half through their equators. Set a strainer over a medium-size bowl and gently squeeze the seeds and gel into the strainer; stir to release the juices, let drain, and then discard the seeds. Use a sharp knife to chop the tomatoes as finely as possible. Transfer the minced tomatoes to the strainer, stir in a little salt, and let drain for 10 minutes or so, stirring now and then. The pulp that remains in the strainer is the concassé. The juice that has drained into the bowl, sometimes called tomato water, is delicious; it can be used to make a Bloody Mary or in Sunday Morning Miracle (page 44).

BEST USES

Tomato salad; tomato and onion salad; BLT salad; bread salad; warm green beans, especially Romano-type beans; risotto, especially olive risotto; grilled flat fish such as flounder

WARM FAVA VINAIGRETTE

SAVORY

WARM

FRAGRANT

For three or four weeks in mid to late spring, there's an abundance of fresh fava beans in most farmers' markets and some independent supermarkets. If you love fresh young favas, it is a glorious time. I enjoy them in simple pasta dishes, folded into creamy risottos, on bruschetta slathered with fresh sheep's milk ricotta, and in this lovely seasonal vinaigrette.

MAKES ABOUT 1½ CUPS

Olive oil
1 shallot, minced
2 garlic cloves, minced
Kosher salt
1 cup fresh shelled, blanched, and peeled fava beans (see Note page 76)
2 tablespoons best-quality white wine vinegar, such as Banyuls
1 tablespoon freshly squeezed lemon juice
6 tablespoons extra-virgin olive oil
Black pepper in a mill
1 teaspoon fresh thyme or snipped fresh chives

Pour a little olive oil into a small sauté pan set over medium-low heat, add the shallot, and sauté until soft and fragrant, about 7 minutes. Add the garlic and sauté for 2 minutes more. Season with salt.

Add the favas, vinegar, lemon juice, and olive oil; heat through but do not let the mixture boil. Stir, taste, and correct for salt. Season with several generous turns of black pepper.

Remove from the heat and stir in the thyme. Use immediately.

RECIPE CONTINUES

Note: You'll need 2 to 2 1/2 pounds of fresh favas to get 1 cup of fava beans. First, shell the peas as you would English peas or any other shell bean. To peel them, fill a saucepan half-full with water, add a generous pinch of salt, and bring to a boil over high heat. Add the shelled beans and simmer for 1 1/2 minutes, or 2 minutes if the beans are large. Drain and refresh in cool water. When the beans are cool enough to handle, remove the rubbery skins. This is best done by making a small tear in the skin and then squeezing out the bean.

BEST USES

Asparagus salad; oven-roasted asparagus; oven-roasted asparagus with poached eggs; fresh artichoke salad; farro salad; rice salad; omelets and frittatas

WARM BACON-MAPLE VINAIGRETTE

SAVORY

SWEET

FRAGRANT

WARM

TANGY

When was it that the country went crazy for bacon? I think it was about the time, or just after, my book celebrating the bacon, lettuce, and tomato sandwich—*The BLT Cookbook* (William Morrow, 2003)—was published, in late spring 2003. Right about the same time, a man founded the first Bacon-of-the-Month Club, and soon you could find everything from bacon lip gloss and bacon-flavored vodka to Baconnaise, a flavored mayonnaise that actually contains no pork, let alone any bacon of any kind. I've had chocolate-coated bacon lollipops, bacon ice cream, candied bacon, and even bacon cupcakes. Yet have we tired of bacon? No. Even many vegetarians find it irresistible. Shortly after appearing on the *Today* show to promote the book, I received an email from a vegetarian declaring her love for the stuff. Bacon is not meat, she said; bacon is fat, which in her mind was a good thing (I agree). Strict vegetarians may want to skip over this recipe, though, as there is no real substitute for bacon.

MAKES ABOUT ½ CUP

1 shallot, minced
2 garlic cloves, minced
Kosher salt
2 tablespoons sherry vinegar
3 bacon slices, cut in half crosswise
4 to 6 tablespoons extra-virgin olive oil
1 tablespoon pure maple syrup
Black pepper in a mill
1 tablespoon chopped fresh Italian parsley

Put the shallot and garlic in a small bowl, season with salt, and add the vinegar. Set aside.

RECIPE CONTINUES

In a medium sauté pan, cook the bacon over medium heat until it is completely crisp. Transfer to paper towels or a brown paper bag to drain.

Pour off all but 2 tablespoons of the bacon fat from the pan, return the pan to low heat, and add the vinegar mixture. Simmer for about 1 minute. Add 4 tablespoons of the olive oil and the maple syrup and heat through. Stir, season generously with black pepper, then taste and correct for salt, oil, and acid. Heat through again, remove from the heat, and add the Italian parsley.

Crumble the bacon and add it to the finished vinaigrette. Use immediately, while the vinaigrette is hot.

Variation

SAVORY BACON VINAIGRETTE: Omit the maple syrup and taste carefully for acid. Use this on sliced tomato salad, tomato and mozzarella or burrata salad, bread salad with tomatoes and olives, warm potato salad, or risotto.

BEST USES

Shredded red leaf lettuce; spinach salad; cherry tomato salad; pasta salads; roasted corn salad or grilled corn on the cob; fried or poached eggs

CHAPTER 2

Around
the World

If there is a cuisine that doesn't employ the irresistible combination of salt, fat, and acid to enliven and brighten vegetables, grains, seafood, poultry, and meats, I've not yet found it. The world is a kaleidoscope of condiments—some that evolved specifically as dressings for salads, others that didn't but perform the duty so deliciously that I have included them here. The recipes in this chapter are, primarily, inspired by my travels and by my love of the full-flavored cuisines of India and Southeast Asia, Mexico and South America, the Mediterranean, the Middle East, and North Africa.

India, the site of my first adventure outside my native California, has its yogurt-based raitas, which I've loved since my first taste. The Middle East enjoys myriad variations of garlic, lemon, olive oil, herbs, and spices (flavor combinations that also appear in Argentina), not to mention the simple yogurt and tahini mixtures that are indescribably good; you've got to try them to understand. The Yogurt-Tahini Dressing (page 99) in this chapter is an easy and delicious way to begin.

Asia employs both soy sauce and fish sauce in an array of condiments used in vegetable, noodle, and meat salads. Re-creating Japanese dressings at home presents the biggest challenge, because most Japanese vinaigrettes contain a bit of dashi (a group of broths and stocks), hardly a staple in Western kitchens. But I have included a simple and yummy Japanese soy-lime dressing here. Many Asian dressings also feature a burst of fire from fresh or dried chiles, as do many of the sauces of Mexico.

Food is our common ground, a universal experience.

—James Beard

In food, as in death, we feel the essential brotherhood of man.

—Vietnamese proverb

ZING! SOY-LIME DRESSING

SAVORY

TANGY

RICH

This is likely the easiest dressing you'll ever make. It is also surprisingly delicious, more than a simple sum of its parts. I've been making it for decades and have never grown tired of it.

It's interesting that this recipe is so simple, because Japanese cuisine, including salad dressings, is highly codified, with essential ingredients that require special effort to secure outside of Japan and considerable experience to use adeptly. Many Japanese recipes, including vinaigrettes, have a bit of dashi (a group of broths and stocks); the most traditional version is made with kombu, a type of kelp, and bonito, a type of tuna. Without it, it is often impossible to create authentic Japanese flavors.

MAKES ABOUT ½ CUP

6 tablespoons sushi-quality soy sauce
2 tablespoons freshly squeezed lime juice

Put the soy sauce in a small serving bowl, add the lime juice, stir, and serve.

Variations

SPICY SOY-LIME DRESSING: Add 1/2 teaspoon crushed red pepper flakes.

RICH SOY-LIME DRESSING: Add 1 tablespoon toasted sesame oil and 1 tablespoon toasted sesame seeds.

BEST USES

Seaweed salad; seaweed and noodle salad; as a dip for toasted nori; grilled shrimp with thinly sliced cucumber; grilled beef salad

SAVORY

TANGY

HOT

When I make a Thai meat salad, I leave the sesame seeds out of this dressing and sprinkle them over the salad just before serving it.

MAKES ABOUT ½ CUP

5 large garlic cloves, minced

5 serranos or similar green chiles, seeded and minced

4 teaspoons sugar

2 tablespoons Thai fish sauce, such as Golden Boy brand

¼ cup freshly squeezed lime juice

2 teaspoons white sesame seeds, lightly toasted (optional)

Put the garlic and chiles in a small glass bowl, add the sugar, fish sauce, and lime juice, and stir for a few seconds, until the sugar is dissolved. Add the sesame seeds, if using. Use immediately, or refrigerate, covered, for up to 4 days.

BEST USES

Thai grilled beef salad; Thai larb (with ground chicken, ground pork, or ground duck); grilled squid; vegetable slaw; glass noodle salad; sliced cucumbers and onions

MINA'S TEARS: ABSINTHE, HONEYDEW, AND CUCUMBER DRESSING

SAVORY

SWEET

FRAGRANT

COOL

At the Francis Ford Coppola Winery, about half an hour from my home in west Sonoma County, a display case with three of the Oscar-winning costumes from *Bram Stoker's Dracula* sits opposite the bar. Although none of Mina's dresses are displayed, there are photos of them. I used to sit at the bar wishing they had absinthe. "Soon," the bartenders would tell me, and then my imagination would gallop away. That's how this fragrant dressing got its name. Mina's Tears, I thought one evening as I sipped a glass of Sofia sparkling wine. If you've seen the movie, you understand the inspiration. This dressing must be tasted as you make it, as absinthe varies wildly from brand to brand. Sugar and lime juice, especially, should be added in small amounts to boost and round out any flavors that seem to fall flat on the palate.

MAKES ABOUT 1 CUP

½ cup honeydew melon juice (see Note page 87)
¼ cup cucumber juice (see Note page 95)
3 tablespoons absinthe
1 teaspoon sugar, plus more to taste
Generous pinch of kosher salt
Squeeze of lime juice (optional)
8 to 10 fresh mint leaves, gently torn into medium-size pieces

Put the melon juice, cucumber juice, and absinthe in a small bowl, add the sugar and salt, and stir to dissolve. Taste, and squeeze in a bit of lime juice if needed to boost the flavor, add the mint, cover, and refrigerate for at least 30 minutes and up to 3 hours.

RECIPE CONTINUES

Note: For ¹/₂ cup honeydew juice, you'll need about 1¹/₂ cups diced melon. Simply cut open a melon, scoop out the flesh, and cut it into small dice. Put the diced melon in a strainer set over a deep bowl and stir it now and then as it drains; it will take 20 to 30 minutes for the melon to release most of its juice. Occasionally crush the melon gently with the side of spoon, but do not press it through the strainer. Strain the juice before using.

BEST USES

The Best Fruit Salad Ever (page 142); salad of melon (any), red onion, and prosciutto; grilled green grapes over frisée and feta and topped with Marcona almonds; mixed with sparkling wine, for an unusual and refreshing cocktail

SAVORY

TANGY

FRAGRANT

SPICY

Chimichurri is a condiment that is traditionally served in Argentina with *asa-dos*, or grilled meats. It is also sometimes thinned and used as a marinade for meats while they are cooking. Once you've had it on a juicy rare rib-eye steak, you will never want to be without it. Chimichurri's popularity has spread throughout South America, Central America, and Mexico and there are many variations, some that call for vinegar or wine instead of lemon juice and many that do not include cilantro. Some Argentine versions are made with dried parsley but with good Italian parsley so readily available these days, it is not necessary to rely on dried, which lacks the full flavor of fresh.

MAKES ABOUT 1 ½ CUPS

2 small shallots, minced

4 garlic cloves, minced

½ cup fresh Italian parsley, minced

½ cup fresh cilantro, minced

1 teaspoon fresh thyme, minced

1 teaspoon fresh oregano, minced

1 teaspoon smoked paprika (optional)

Juice of 1 lemon, plus more to taste

Kosher salt

Black pepper in a mill

Pinch or two of red pepper flakes

2 fresh bay leaves, pounded

¾ to 1 cup extra-virgin olive oil

Put the shallots, garlic, parsley, cilantro, thyme, oregano, paprika (if using), and lemon juice in a medium bowl and stir. Season generously with salt and pepper, and add a generous pinch or two, depending on your preference, of red pepper flakes. Tuck the pounded bay leaves into the sauce, cover, and chill for about 2 hours.

Remove the sauce from the refrigerator; use tongs to remove and discard the bay leaves. Stir in the olive oil, taste, and correct for acid and salt as needed. Use immediately, or refrigerate, covered, for up to 2 days.

BEST USES

Farro salad; quinoa salad; grilled vegetable salad; sliced onion salad; grilled eggplant and zucchini salad; sliced tomato salad; roasted chicken salad; grilled shrimp salad; grilled meat, especially rare beef; whole roasted lamb; whole roasted goat

ITALIAN-STYLE SALSA VERDE

SAVORY

TANGY

FRAGRANT

SPICY

Although Italian salsa verde is traditionally considered a condiment rather than a salad dressing, it is one of the best dressings in the world for certain types of salads, especially those made with grains, rice, or tiny pasta. Barley, farro, brown rice, or Israeli couscous dressed with nothing more than this is absolutely extraordinary. It is also delicious with a wide range of other foods, from raw zucchini sliced into thin ribbons to grilled meats. For more traditional versions, see the variations on page 92.

MAKES ABOUT 2 CUPS

4 cups loosely packed fresh Italian parsley, chopped

6 scallions, white and pale green parts only, very thinly sliced

1 medium cucumber, peeled, seeded, and cut into small dice

5 garlic cloves, minced

2 tablespoons capers, drained and minced, or 2 tablespoons brined
    green peppercorns, drained

1 tablespoon Dijon mustard

Grated zest of 2 lemons

¼ cup freshly squeezed lemon juice

Kosher salt

⅔ cup extra-virgin olive oil, plus more to taste

Black pepper in a mill

Put the parsley, scallions, cucumber, garlic, and capers in a medium bowl and toss with a fork.

Put the mustard, lemon zest, and lemon juice in a small bowl, season generously with salt, and stir in the olive oil. Season with several turns of black pepper and pour over the parsley mixture. Taste, and correct for salt and acid as needed. Cover and let sit

RECIPE CONTINUES

for 30 minutes before using. Although salsa verde is best when first made, it can be refrigerated, covered, for up to 3 days.

Variations

TRADITIONAL SALSA VERDE TO SERVE WITH MEAT: Omit the scallions, cucumber, and lemon juice. Add 2 tablespoons anchovy paste or 12 anchovy fillets, mashed, along with the mustard and 2 to 3 tablespoons (to taste) of red wine vinegar.

TRADITIONAL SALSA VERDE TO SERVE WITH FISH: Omit the scallions and cucumber. Add 2 tablespoons anchovy paste or 12 anchovy fillets, mashed, along with the mustard and lemon juice.

BEST USES

Raw zucchini ribbons; grilled radicchio; grilled asparagus; grilled cabbage wedges; whole roasted cauliflower; farro salad; barley salad; pasta salad with small pasta, such as acini di pepe; bread salad; grilled fish, poultry, and beef; pulled pork sandwiches

---

HARISSA SAUCE

Harissa is essential to Moroccan cuisine. The name really refers to two things: a paste and a sauce made from that paste. The paste keeps for quite some time in the refrigerator, and it is simple to prepare the sauce when you have the paste on hand. In a pinch, you can even buy harissa paste in a tube, can, or jar; I recommend DEA brand in a tube. There are many versions, some containing only garlic and chiles, others made with a range of both fragrant and hot spices; my homemade version is moderately hot. Typically served with tagines and couscous, harissa makes an extraordinary dressing for a huge array of vegetable, seafood, and meat salads.

MAKES ABOUT ½ CUP

2 tablespoons Harissa Paste (page 94, or use store-bought),
    plus more to taste
2 tablespoons freshly squeezed lemon juice
3 tablespoons extra-virgin olive oil
Warm water or chicken stock, as needed
1 tablespoon minced fresh cilantro
1 tablespoon minced fresh Italian parsley
Kosher salt, if needed

RECIPE CONTINUES

BEST USES

Couscous salad; grilled zucchini and carrots; grain (especially farro and barley) salad; leafy greens with grilled lamb; bread salad with merguez and grilled zucchini; roasted sweet and hot peppers, with or without fresh chèvre; grilled eggplant with Yogurt-Tahini Dressing (page 99)

Put the harissa paste in a small bowl and stir in the lemon juice and olive oil. Taste, and correct for acid, olive oil, and heat as needed.

Thin to your preferred consistency with a little warm water or chicken stock. Stir in the cilantro and parsley, stir, taste, and correct for salt as needed (usually, the salt in the harissa is sufficient). The sauce is best used the day it is made.

HARISSA PASTE

MAKES ABOUT ⅔ CUP

1½ ounces dried red chiles, preferably ancho
1 tablespoon cumin seeds, lightly toasted
2 teaspoons coriander seeds
1 teaspoon caraway seeds
6 garlic cloves, crushed
2 teaspoons kosher salt, plus more as needed
½ cup olive oil

Heat a heavy pan—cast iron is ideal—over high heat. Add the chiles and toast, turning frequently, until they puff up with fragrant steam; transfer to a work surface to cool. When they're cool enough to handle, remove the stems and seed cores. Use a sharp knife to scrape the meat from the skin, but don't worry if you can't remove all the skin; it is okay to use some of it.

Grind the cumin, coriander, and caraway seeds in an electric spice grinder or suribachi (see page 12).

Put the chiles, ground seeds, garlic, salt, and olive oil in the work bowl of a food processor and pulse until the ingredients form a very thick smooth paste. Taste, and if the paste tastes flat, add a little more salt and pulse again. Transfer to a small wide-mouthed Mason jar and store, covered, in the refrigerator for up to 2 weeks.

COOL AS A CUCUMBER

SAVORY

FRAGRANT

COOL

Is this a vinaigrette? Sort of. Yet it is so delicate and fragile that I hesitate to use the moniker. It is best in the dog days of summer, when the air is perfectly still and even nights are hot.

MAKES ABOUT ¾ CUP

1 tablespoon minced red onion
½ cup strained cucumber juice (see Note)
2 tablespoons freshly squeezed lemon juice
Kosher salt
2 teaspoons minced fresh chives
8 to 10 fresh mint leaves, shredded (optional)
3 to 4 tablespoons peanut oil or mild olive oil

Put the onion in a small bowl or small wide-mouthed Mason jar, add the cucumber juice and lemon juice, and let sit for 15 to 20 minutes.

Season with a little kosher salt, add the chives and mint (if using), and pour in the peanut oil or olive oil. Stir or shake, taste, and correct for salt and acid as needed. Cover and refrigerate for at least 30 minutes and as long as 3 hours. This light, delicate dressing is best the day it is made.

Note: To make cucumber juice, peel and mince a large slicing (not pickling) cucumber. Put it into a medium strainer set over a deep bowl, add a teaspoon of salt, and stir now and then for 30 minutes.

BEST USES

Light pasta salad; Little Gem lettuce with bay shrimp or feta cheese; cucumber and celery salad; watercress salad; salad of green melon and lemon cucumbers

SAVORY

TANGY

FRAGRANT

SPICY

Chermoula is a traditional condiment found throughout Algeria, Tunisia, and Morocco. There are myriad variations—some with tomatoes, some with roasted sweet peppers, some with saffron and ginger—and all are delicious. In Morocco, Chermoula is used as both a marinade and a condiment with nearly all types of fish and shellfish. It makes a wonderful dressing for vegetable, bread, potato, or egg salads, as well as salads with mozzarella or burrata.

MAKES ABOUT 1 ¼ CUPS

3 or 4 garlic cloves, peeled

Kosher salt

1 cup lightly packed fresh cilantro, chopped

½ cup lightly packed fresh Italian parsley, chopped

2 teaspoons sweet paprika, preferably Spanish

1 teaspoon hot paprika, preferably Spanish

2 teaspoons ground cumin

1 teaspoon chipotle chile powder or *piment d'Espelette*

Juice of 2 lemons

½ cup extra-virgin olive oil, plus more to taste

Put the garlic in a suribachi (see page 12) or mortar, sprinkle lightly with salt, and use a wooden pestle to crush the garlic into a paste. Add the cilantro and parsley and continue to grind with the wooden pestle until a uniform puree is formed. Add both paprikas, cumin, and chipotle powder, and stir in the lemon juice.

Season with salt and stir in the olive oil. Taste, and correct for salt and acid as needed. Cover and chill; remove from the refrigerator 30 minutes before using. Chermoula will keep up to 2 days in the refrigerator, but it is best the day it is made.

RECIPE CONTINUES

Variations

PRESERVED LEMON CHERMOULA: Use the juice of a single lemon and add 2 tablespoons minced preserved lemon (commercial or homemade).

SMOKY CHERMOULA: Replace the sweet paprika and hot paprika with 1 tablespoon smoked paprika.

FRAGRANT CHERMOULA: Put a generous pinch of saffron threads into a small bowl, add 1 teaspoon hot water, swirl, and let rest for a few minutes. Add the saffron and its liquid and 2 teaspoons grated fresh ginger to the garlic paste before adding the cilantro and parsley.

BEST USES

Carrot salad; zucchini salad; grilled eggplant; sliced tomato and mozzarella salad; fresh greens with burrata; sausage (especially merguez) and bread salad; potato salad; chickpea and rice salad; deviled eggs; summer vegetable soup; grilled chicken or beef

YOGURT-TAHINI DRESSING

SAVORY

TANGY

RICH

CREAMY

This recipe evolved from a traditional Lebanese dish of chickpeas and toasted lavash slathered with this sauce and topped with hot olive oil and pine nuts—a sort of Middle Eastern nachos. It is very easy to make, it keeps well, and both omnivores and vegetarians love it.

MAKES ABOUT 1 CUP

1 cup plain whole-milk yogurt

1 tablespoon raw sesame tahini

1 teaspoon kosher salt

1 teaspoon freshly squeezed lemon juice

1 tablespoon minced fresh cilantro or mint

Put the yogurt in a small bowl, add the tahini, and mix with a small whisk until very smooth.

Put the salt in one spot on top of the mixture, and pour the lemon juice on top of it so it will dissolve the salt; give it a minute or two to dissolve. Whisk, and fold in the cilantro. Use immediately, or refrigerate, covered, for up to 10 days.

BEST USES

Grilled vegetables, especially eggplant, carrots, zucchini, and asparagus, often with Harissa Sauce (page 93) as well; grilled sausages, especially merguez and other lamb sausages; as a dip for toasted pita chips; rice and roasted vegetable salads

RAITA WITH MANY VARIATIONS

SAVORY

SWEET

TANGY

FRAGRANT

SPICY

HOT

CREAMY

Traditionally, raita is served with Indian curries and other savory Indian dishes, as part of the kaleidoscope of condiments that makes Indian cuisine so compelling. But a raita need not be limited to Indian foods; it is delicious with a huge array of salads and as a topping for many soups. This template recipe is designed to be customized with your flavoring ingredients of choice, suggestions for which follow.

MAKES ABOUT 1½ CUPS

1 cup plain whole-milk yogurt
Flavoring ingredients of choice (see below)
Kosher salt
Black or white pepper in a mill

Put the yogurt in a medium bowl, prepare and add the flavoring ingredients you've chosen, and mix together.

Taste, season with salt and pepper, and mix well. Use immediately, or refrigerate, covered, for up to 3 days.

Ingredient Combinations

CILANTRO-MINT RAITA: Add ¼ cup chopped fresh cilantro, 1 tablespoon shredded mint, 1 minced serrano chile, 1 minced garlic clove, and 1 teaspoon grated fresh ginger to the yogurt.

RADISH RAITA: Add 1 bunch (8 to 10) radishes cut into small dice, 2 tablespoons minced red onion, 1 minced garlic clove, and ½ minced serrano chile to the yogurt.

CELERY RAITA: Trim 2 large celery ribs and slice them very thin on the diagonal; cut the slices in half or in thirds if particularly wide. Add sliced celery, 1 teaspoon celery seeds, 1 teaspoon brined green peppercorns, ½ teaspoon crushed coriander seeds, 2 shredded curry leaves (if available), and 1 tablespoon chopped Italian parsley or cilantro to the yogurt.

CARROT RAITA: Cut a smallish carrot into thin julienne and simmer it in boiling salted water until just barely tender, 2 to 3 minutes. Drain and cool. Add the carrots, 1 minced garlic clove, the grated zest of 1 lemon, 1 teaspoon ground cumin, 1 teaspoon toasted cumin seeds, and $1/2$ teaspoon toasted mustard seeds to the yogurt.

FENNEL RAITA: Add $1/2$ cup grated fennel bulb, 1 tablespoon minced red onion, 2 teaspoons minced fennel fronds, 1 teaspoon toasted fennel seeds, 1 teaspoon toasted fennel pollen (if available), and 6 to 8 shredded fresh mint leaves to the yogurt.

GARLIC RAITA: Add 6 to 8 minced garlic cloves, 1 minced serrano or jalapeño chile (remove the seeds for a milder taste), and 2 tablespoons chopped fresh cilantro to the yogurt. Season with salt, stir well, and sprinkle with 1 teaspoon or so of garam masala (a mixture of black and white pepper, cardamom, cinnamon, cloves, coriander, cumin, mace, nutmeg, and sometimes star anise) before serving.

BEET RAITA: Roast 3 small or 2 medium red beets until tender. Cool, peel, and cut into very thin julienne. Add the beets, 2 tablespoons chopped fresh cilantro, 1 tablespoon shredded fresh mint, and 1 teaspoon sugar to the yogurt.

PINEAPPLE RAITA: Add $1/2$ cup diced fresh pineapple, 1 small minced shallot, $1/2$ small minced serrano chile, 1 tablespoon chopped fresh cilantro, $1/2$ teaspoon crushed cardamom seeds, and $1/2$ teaspoon toasted cumin seeds.

BEST USES

Salad of chickpeas, ditalini, and celery; salad of steamed carrots and zucchini; grilled eggplant; grilled cabbage wedges; grilled iceberg lettuce wedges with halved cherry tomatoes; roasted beet salad; soup of kale and radish greens (Radish Raita); sliced tomato salad (Cilantro-Mint Raita, Celery Raita); roasted chicken salad; fruit salad (Pineapple Raita)

SAVORY

TANGY

SPICY

CREAMY

In hot weather, I like to entertain with a salsa bar, and I've done it many times for both small and large gatherings. Along with the selection of salsas, I always include something creamy as a contrast, and it's usually this spicy crema. I like a smooth mixture and achieve it by pureeing chiles, garlic, and cilantro with a small amount of the crema—not the full quantity, so as to retain the voluptuous texture.

MAKES ABOUT 3 CUPS

2 cups Mexican crema or best-quality sour cream
1 or 2 serrano or jalapeño chiles, chopped
2 or 3 garlic cloves, crushed
1 cup loosely packed fresh cilantro, chopped
Kosher salt
1 tablespoon freshly squeezed lime juice, plus more as needed
1 cup crème fraîche
Black pepper in a mill

Put about $1/2$ cup of the crema in the work bowl (preferably a small work bowl) of a food processor fitted with a metal blade. Put the rest of the crema in a medium bowl and set aside.

Add the serranos, garlic, cilantro, and several generous pinches of salt to the bowl of the food processor and pulse several times, until very smooth. Add the lime juice and pulse again.

Pour the mixture into the bowl with the remaining crema, using a rubber spatula to scrape the sides of the work bowl. Add the crème fraîche and whisk thoroughly until the mixture is smooth and uniform. Taste, and correct for salt and acid as needed.

Season with several turns of black pepper, transfer to a serving bowl, cover, and refrigerate for at least 1 hour, or until thoroughly chilled. Use immediately, or refrigerate, covered, for up to 2 days.

BEST USES

Iceberg and Little Gem lettuce wedges; as a dip with radishes, jicama, celery, carrots, and tortilla chips; roasted vegetable salad; avocado salad; taco salad; grilled cabbage wedges; Mexican tortas; alongside queso fundido

AVOCADO AND GREEN PEPPERCORN CREAM

Early one morning in the mid 1980s, I accompanied some friends while they took their VW bus to be repaired at a dealership on the outskirts of La Paz, in central Baja California. As we left to walk into town to wait, we spotted a young boy, possibly in his early teens, wheeling a cart under a tree across from the shop. He quickly unfolded the equipment and before long was serving carnitas tacos that couldn't have been simpler or more delicious. Two very small corn tortillas, heated on a propane-fired grill, were topped with chunks of succulent meat and then slathered with the most extraordinary avocado sauce I'd ever tasted. I stood there in the morning sun and devoured five tacos, stopping only for the sake of decorum. I've been making a version of that sauce ever since, and this one is my current favorite.

MAKES ABOUT 1 ½ CUPS

1 large or 2 medium ripe Hass avocados, pitted, peeled, and
    cut in cubes
½ serrano or jalapeño chile
1 teaspoon brined green peppercorns
2 tablespoons freshly squeezed lime juice
2 tablespoons water, plus more as needed
1 teaspoon kosher salt, plus more to taste
Black pepper in a mill
2 tablespoons chopped fresh cilantro

Put the avocado in the work bowl of a food processor (preferably a small work bowl) fitted with a metal blade. If you like a lot of heat, chop the chile without seeding it. For a milder flavor, remove the seeds and chop. Add to the work bowl, along with the green peppercorns, lime juice, water, salt, and several generous turns of black pepper. Pulse several times and then process until the mixture is quite smooth.

Taste, correct for salt as needed, and, if necessary, adjust for texture by adding another teaspoon or two of water if it seems too thick. Transfer to a small bowl and fold in the cilantro. Use immediately, or refrigerate, covered, for up to 3 days.

BEST USES

Little Gem or iceberg lettuce wedges topped with diced celery, bay shrimp, or crumbled bacon; salad greens and grilled shrimp; as a dip with radishes, carrots, celery, jicama, cherry tomatoes, and tortilla chips; taco salads; chilled cucumber soup

CHAPTER 3

Classically Creamy

Most creamy salad dressings are based, at least in part, on mayonnaise, one of the world's most widely used mother sauces, a foundation upon which dozens of other condiments are built. It is the classic cold emulsion and, unless you hate it, is as essential a pantry ingredient as, say, olive oil or vinegar, or nearly so. It is also easy to make.

Today, mayonnaise has a French pedigree, though its historic roots extend into Spain and Catalonia; mayonnaise-based sauces have evolved from both regions. From Catalonia, we have romesco, with almonds, tomatoes, and peppers; and alioli, a kissing cousin of the classic Provençal garlic mayonnaise, aioli. France also gives us rouille, similar to aioli but spiked with saffron and, traditionally, monkfish liver and served with bouillabaisse; and rémoulade, today also a signature sauce of New Orleans.

The popularity of mayonnaise has spread—ha!—worldwide. It is used to make tartar sauce, an essential accompaniment, along with malt vinegar, to fish and chips. Walnut prawns, a dish found in Chinese restaurants throughout the United States, is dressed with mayonnaise sweetened with honey because, as restaurateurs will tell you if you ask, "Americans love mayonnaise." Russian dressing and similar Thousand Island dressing both require mayonnaise, and if you deconstruct many of the dipping and spreading sauces popular in American fast-food joints, you'll find mayonnaise or a close equivalent.

On its own, mayonnaise is absolutely essential in potato salad, egg salad, coleslaw, and Hawaiian mac salad. It is also the traditional condiment with *frites*—a.k.a. French fries—in France and Belgium. "*Frites avec sauce*" is how you order; the nature of the sauce is understood.

Other ingredients sometimes contribute their creamy qualities to salad dressings, either alone, as in Avocado and Green Peppercorn Cream (page 104), or in tandem with mayonnaise, as in this chapter's ranch dressings (pages 122 and 124) and Best Louis Dressing in the World (page 126), with its light, voluptuous texture created by whipped cream.

Mayonnaise, real mayonnaise, good mayonnaise, is something I can dream of any time, almost, and not because I ate it when I was little but because I did not. My maternal grandmother, whose Victorian neuroses dictated our family table tastes until I was about twelve, found salads generally suspect.

—M. F. K. Fisher, *With Bold Knife & Fork* (1969)

CAESAR SALAD-STYLE ANCHOVY DRESSING

SAVORY

TANGY

SPICY

CREAMY

Although traditional Caesar salad is made by adding ingredients one at a time to the prepared lettuce, this version is quite similar to the resulting dressing and can be used to make delicious Caesar salad. Simply turn small inner romaine leaves in the dressing and then top them with garlicky croutons.

MAKES ABOUT 1 CUP

3 garlic cloves, crushed
3 to 4 oil-packed anchovy fillets, drained
1 egg yolk, from a backyard or pastured hen
1 tablespoon Dijon mustard
Juice of 1 lemon, plus more as needed
¾ cup extra-virgin olive oil
¼ cup freshly grated Parmigiano-Reggiano cheese
Black pepper in a mill
Kosher salt

Put the garlic in a suribachi (see page 12) or mortar, add the anchovies, and use a wooden pestle to crush together into a paste. Add the egg yolk, mix well, and then stir in the mustard and lemon juice. Use a small whisk or fork to stir in the olive oil and fold in the cheese. Season generously with black pepper.

Taste the dressing, and if it is a bit flat, add two or three generous pinches of salt, squeeze some lemon juice on top of the salt so that it dissolves, and stir into the dressing. Use immediately, or refrigerate, covered, for up to 3 days.

Note: If you have a small food processor, you can use it to make this dressing. To do so, first pound the garlic in a suribachi or mortar and transfer it to the work bowl of the processor. Add the anchovies and mustard, pulse, add the egg yolk, and season with salt. Pulse a few times and then, with the machine operating, slowly drizzle in the olive oil.

Taste, and if it needs salt, add several pinches on top of the dressing. Drizzle the lemon juice on top. Pulse 2 or 3 times. Add the cheese and several turns of black pepper, pulse, and transfer to a bowl. Use immediately, or refrigerate, covered, for up to 3 days.

BEST USES

Simple green salad; inner leaves of romaine; roasted chicken salad; as a dip with sliced radishes, celery, and cucumbers

SAVORY

CREAMY

Mayonnaise is one of the classic mother sauces, a base upon which many other classic sauces are built. Although most of us do not bother to make mayonnaise at home, it is easy to do and the results are excellent. This recipe can easily be doubled or even tripled, provided you follow the simple ratio of 1 egg yolk to 1 cup oil. You can make mayonnaise with less oil—say $2/3$ or $3/4$ cup—if that is all you need, but a single yolk will not absorb more than 1 cup.

MAKES ABOUT 1¼ CUPS

1 large or jumbo egg yolk, from a backyard or pastured hen
Generous pinch of kosher salt
1 teaspoon freshly squeezed lemon juice or white wine vinegar, plus
   more to taste
1 cup mild olive oil

Put the egg yolk in a small mixing bowl, season with salt, and whisk until very smooth and thick. Add the lemon juice or vinegar and mix again.

Begin adding the olive oil a few drops at a time, mixing thoroughly after each addition. As the emulsion forms, gradually increase the quantity of oil you add to a small but steady drizzle.

Taste and correct for salt and acid as needed. If the mayonnaise is too thick for you, thin with 1 or 2 teaspoons of water. Use immediately, or refrigerate, covered, for up to 4 days.

Variations

MUSTARD MAYONNAISE: Stir in 2 tablespoons of your favorite mustard. Use on grilled chicken and grilled salmon salad and sandwiches.

RASPBERRY MAYONNAISE: Add about 1 teaspoon sugar to the egg yolk and replace the lemon juice with 1 tablespoon low-acid raspberry vinegar. This is delicious in coleslaw.

BLUEBERRY MAYONNAISE: Add 1 teaspoon sugar and a generous pinch of ground cloves to the egg yolk and replace the lemon juice with 1 tablespoon low-acid blueberry vinegar. This is delicious over sautéed chicken livers or with blueberry and lettuce salad.

TAPENADE MAYONNAISE: Stir 2 tablespoons commercial or homemade tapenade into the mayonnaise. Use on sandwiches, with steamed or boiled artichokes, and with grilled salmon.

HARISSA MAYONNAISE: Stir 2 teaspoons commercial or homemade (page 94) harissa paste into the finished mayonnaise, along with 1 tablespoon each chopped fresh cilantro and chopped Italian parsley.

BEST USES

Chilled artichokes; potato salad; egg salad; deviled eggs; Hawaiian macaroni salad; vegetable slaw; vegetable slaw with fruit (raspberry, blueberry, apple); BLT salad; French fries; as a base for other sauces and dressings

TRUE AIOLI

SAVORY

TANGY

SPICY

CREAMY

When you see recipes for aioli that call for one or two cloves of garlic, understand that they have been adapted for Americans. True Provençal aioli has much more garlic than just a clove or two. That said, feel free to adjust this recipe to suit your taste—though my feeling is, if you don't like garlic, just make mayonnaise.

You can make aioli in a food processor, just as you can mayonnaise, but it is more voluptuous when made by hand. Having the right equipment (see page 12) is essential, especially if you want to enjoy the process. There is one exception: In very hot weather, make both mayonnaise and aioli in a food processor, as it creates a more stable emulsion that can stand up to high temperatures without separating. (And it goes without saying that these and similar sauces should not spend much time in the heat.)

MAKES ABOUT 2½ CUPS

1 large or 2 medium garlic bulbs, cloves separated and peeled
Kosher salt
2 large or jumbo egg yolks, from a backyard or pastured hen
Pinch of *piment d'Espelette*, *paprika picante*, or other ground hot pepper
2 cups best-quality extra-virgin olive oil
2 to 3 teaspoons hot water, as needed
½ lemon, as needed

Set the garlic cloves on a work surface and use the flat side of a broad knife to crush them one at a time. Put the crushed cloves in a suribachi (see page 12) or mortar, sprinkle with salt, and use a sturdy wooden pestle to grind and pound them into a paste. When the garlic is nearly liquefied, add the egg yolks and pinch of *piment d'Espelette* and mix until it is smooth and very thick. Use a small rubber spatula to remove any garlic paste that clings to the wooden pestle, then set the pestle aside and switch to a whisk, preferably a balloon whisk.

RECIPE CONTINUES

Begin adding the olive oil a few drops at a time, mixing thoroughly after each addition. As the emulsion forms, gradually increase the quantity of oil you add to a small but steady drizzle. If the aioli seems too stiff—it should be smooth, creamy, and thick but not stiff—mix in a little of the hot water to loosen it just slightly.

Let rest, covered, for about 15 minutes, and then taste the aioli. If there is any bitterness or it tastes flat, squeeze the juice of the lemon near the edge of the bowl and sprinkle a few pinches of salt into the pool of juice. Agitate the bowl gently so that the salt dissolves, and then whisk the aioli until smooth. Cover and refrigerate until 30 minutes before serving. Use immediately, or refrigerate, covered, for up to 2 days.

Variations

ROASTED GARLIC AIOLI: Mash 5 or 6 cloves roasted garlic (page 31; omit the thyme) until smooth and add to the egg yolk mixture.

SPICY AIOLI: Stir 1 to 2 tablespoons commercial or homemade (page 94) harissa paste into the finished aioli. Taste and correct for salt and acid.

BEST USES

Grand aioli (fresh vegetables, hard-boiled eggs, and either poached salt cod or stewed octopus); grand aioli with roasted chicken and hot crusty bread; roasted sweet peppers; tuna salad; grilled fresh tuna salad; BLT salad; BLT; avocado salad; chilled artichokes; chicken sandwiches; French fries

CREAMY SESAME-GINGER DRESSING

SWEET

TANGY

SPICY

RICH

CREAMY

There was a sweet Japanese restaurant named Tengu in the town where I lived in the early 1980s that served the most delicious coleslaw: cabbage and onion sliced as thin as thread with a creamy dressing redolent with sesame. Although I knew the owners, language was a barrier and I never got the recipe. This dressing comes close to the taste and whenever I make coleslaw with it I'm reminded of that salad and how I treasured the little place.

MAKES ABOUT 1 ¼ CUPS

1 cup mayonnaise, homemade (page 110) or Best Foods/Hellmann's
    brand
2 tablespoons grated fresh ginger
2 tablespoons toasted sesame oil
1 tablespoon apple cider vinegar or rice vinegar
1 tablespoon freshly squeezed lime juice
2 tablespoons granulated sugar
Kosher salt
2 tablespoons white sesame seeds, toasted until golden brown
Black pepper in a mill

Put the mayonnaise in a medium bowl, add the ginger, sesame oil, vinegar, lime juice, sugar, and several generous pinches of salt, and stir with a small whisk until very smooth. Add the sesame seeds and several turns of black pepper, and stir. Use immediately, or refrigerate, covered, for up to 8 days.

BEST USES

Vegetable slaw with cilantro; rock shrimp salad; pasta salad with fresh corn, fresh peas, and bay shrimp; chicken salad over crispy fried noodles; fish and shellfish sandwiches

BLUE CHEESE DRESSING

SAVORY

TANGY

CREAMY

Although ranch dressing has replaced blue cheese dressing when it comes to popularity, blue cheese dressing is still one of the best additions to a good salad, provided it is well made. This one is simple and easily doubled, and it takes just a couple of minutes to prepare, so there is no reason to make a large amount. If you *do* have some left over, refrigerate it and let it come to room temperature before using it.

I usually make the dressing directly in a salad bowl, as I suggest here, adding lettuce and other ingredients on top of it and then using my hands to turn the greens gently in the dressing. To double the recipe or use in another manner—with sliced tomatoes, for example—mix the dressing in a small bowl.

Point Reyes Original Blue cheese is my usual choice for this dressing, as it is made near where I live, is readily available, and is delicious, with a suggestion of the briny sea air that washes over the pastures where the cows graze. If it is available near you, use it; if not, Maytag is an excellent alternative. For a unique twist, use a smoked blue cheese—there are several available commercially—and enjoy the dressing on sliced tomatoes or grilled cabbage wedges.

MAKES ABOUT ⅓ CUP

½ ounce Maytag blue cheese or comparable blue cheese
1 tablespoon crème fraîche or cultured buttermilk
1 tablespoon freshly squeezed lemon juice
Kosher salt
3 tablespoons extra-virgin olive oil, plus more to taste
Black pepper in a mill
1 tablespoon snipped fresh chives or minced fresh Italian parsley

RECIPE CONTINUES

Put the blue cheese in a medium salad bowl and break it into small pieces. Add the crème fraîche or buttermilk and mix together with a fork; you can mix until it's smooth or leave it chunky, whatever you prefer.

Add the lemon juice and sprinkle several pinches of salt into it; agitate the bowl gently to dissolve the salt. Mix with a fork.

Mix in the olive oil, season with black pepper, taste, and correct for salt as needed. Stir in the chives. Use immediately, or refrigerate, covered, for up to 2 days. Let it come to room temperature before serving.

BEST USES

Butter lettuce salad; butter lettuce salad with sliced red onion and avocado; sliced tomato salad; iceberg wedges; grilled iceberg wedges; grilled cabbage wedges

SAVORY

SPICY

RICH

CREAMY

Indian curry goes in and out of style, like shoulder pads and hem lengths. Enormously popular in the 1950s and 1960s, it enjoyed a resurgence in the 1980s, when curried chicken salad was offered at every hip deli. Yet curry actually refers to a cooking technique—long and slow—and not to the fragrant spices we associate with the name. That said, common usage today refers to taste and not technique.

MAKES ABOUT 1 ¼ CUPS

2 tablespoons olive oil

2 teaspoons minced yellow onion

1 tablespoon hot curry powder

1 teaspoon grated fresh ginger

1 teaspoon cumin seeds, toasted and ground

½ teaspoon ground turmeric

Pinch of cayenne pepper

White pepper in a mill

1 cup mayonnaise, homemade (page 110) or Best Foods/Hellmann's brand

Heat the olive oil in a small sauté pan set over medium-low heat. Add the onion and sauté until it is limp and fragrant, about 7 minutes, stirring frequently so that it does not brown. Add the spices and a couple of turns of white pepper, and cook, stirring constantly, for 2 minutes. Remove the mixture from the heat and let cool.

Put the mayonnaise in a small bowl and fold in the spice mixture. Refrigerate, covered, until well chilled. Use immediately, or refrigerate, covered, for up to 1 week.

BEST USES

Chicken salad, with or without fresh English peas or fava beans; butter lettuce and smoked trout salad; grilled chicken sandwiches

CREAMY FETA AND
GREEN PEPPERCORN DRESSING

SAVORY

TANGY

CREAMY

SPICY

I've long been enamored of brined green peppercorns and often use them in place of capers. If you prefer capers, feel free to use them in this dressing; their inclusion would make for a more traditional dressing.

MAKES ABOUT 1 ¼ CUPS

4 ounces feta cheese, preferably Bulgarian, Greek, or French

1 tablespoon red wine vinegar, plus more to taste

1 tablespoon freshly squeezed lemon juice

3 garlic cloves, minced

1 tablespoon brined green peppercorns, rinsed and drained

1 teaspoon dried Greek oregano

Black pepper in a mill

Kosher salt, as needed

⅓ cup crème fraîche

⅓ cup mayonnaise, homemade (page 110) or Best Foods/Hellmann's brand

⅓ cup extra-virgin olive oil

Put the feta in a medium bowl and use a fork to break it up. Add the vinegar, lemon juice, garlic, peppercorns, and oregano and mix until fairly smooth. Season generously with black pepper, taste, and correct for salt as needed. Fold in the crème fraîche and mayonnaise, followed by the olive oil. Taste again and correct for acid and salt as needed. Cover and let sit for 15 or 20 minutes.

Stir and use immediately, or refrigerate, covered, for up to 3 days. Stir and let come to room temperature before serving.

BEST USES

Greek-style salad; tomato salad; tomato salad with grilled bread; onion salad; warm lentil salad; farro salad; as a dip with cucumbers, carrots, celery, cherry tomatoes, and steamed or boiled artichokes

BIG RANCH DRESSING

SAVORY

TANGY

RICH

CREAMY

Ranch dressing is the most popular commercial salad dressing in America, but that popularity is a bit of a mystery, given that it is so simple to make at home. In addition, homemade versions are better tasting, less expensive, and free of the chemical preservatives found in bottled dressings and packaged mixes. In my version, I use celery seeds in place of dill, which I find overwhelming and unpleasant. This Big Ranch Dressing is good for large families and for those who use ranch dressing frequently.

MAKES ABOUT 2 CUPS

2 teaspoons mustard flour (mustard powder), such as Colman's

2 teaspoons water

1 cup cultured buttermilk

½ cup mayonnaise, homemade (page 110) or Best Foods/Hellmann's brand

¼ cup crème fraîche or sour cream

5 teaspoons freshly squeezed lemon juice

2 teaspoons kosher salt, plus more to taste

1 teaspoon hot paprika, preferably Spanish

1 teaspoon sweet paprika, preferably Spanish

1 teaspoon celery seeds

2 tablespoons chopped fresh Italian parsley

1 tablespoon snipped fresh chives

Black pepper in a mill

Put the mustard flour in a small bowl, add the water, stir until smooth, and let sit for 20 minutes.

Put the buttermilk, mayonnaise, and crème fraîche in a bowl and stir with a whisk until smooth. Add the lemon juice, salt, both paprikas, and celery seeds and whisk again. Add the reconstituted mustard, stir well, and fold in the parsley and chives. Season generously with black pepper, taste, and correct for salt as needed. Pour into a pint jar and use immediately, or refrigerate, covered, for up to 6 days.

BEST USES

Romaine lettuce; tomato and onion salad; as a dip with celery, carrots, radishes, chicken wings, and/or just about anything else you like; sandwiches

LITTLE RANCH DRESSING

SAVORY

TANGY

RICH

CREAMY

Most commercial ranch dressings contain dried onion and garlic. I prefer fresh aromatics, but using them shortens the life of the dressing, hence the smaller yield in this version. This dressing is best used the day it is made, though you can store it overnight without the garlic developing an off flavor (any longer, and it will). If you prefer fresh dill, which is traditional, feel free to use it in place of the celery seed. I find it dominates the other flavors and prefer the milder taste of the celery seed.

MAKES ABOUT ½ CUP

¼ cup cultured buttermilk

1 tablespoon mayonnaise, homemade (page 110) or Best Foods/
    Hellmann's brand

1 tablespoon crème fraîche or sour cream

1 teaspoon Dijon mustard

2 teaspoons minced red onion

1 plump garlic clove, minced

Kosher salt

2 teaspoons freshly squeezed lemon juice

½ teaspoon sweet or hot Spanish paprika

½ teaspoon celery seeds

1 tablespoon minced fresh Italian parsley

1 tablespoon snipped fresh chives

Black pepper in a mill

Put the buttermilk, mayonnaise, crème fraîche, and mustard in a small bowl or small wide-mouthed Mason jar. Stir with a fork or small whisk to blend thoroughly.

Put the onion and garlic in a small suribachi (see page 12) or mortar, season generously with salt, and use a wooden pestle to grind them to a paste. Pour in the lemon juice, swirl to loosen the paste, and add to the buttermilk mixture.

Stir in the paprika, celery seeds, parsley, and chives and season generously with black pepper. Taste, and correct for salt as needed. Cover and refrigerate for 30 minutes to let the flavors marry. Use immediately, or refrigerate, covered, for up to 2 days.

BEST USES

Iceberg lettuce wedges; grilled cabbage wedges; cherry tomato salad; grilled zucchini; also see Best Uses for Big Ranch Dressing (page 123)

SAVORY

SWEET

RICH

CREAMY

I began making this dressing, or a very similar version, when I was still a teenager. Living near San Francisco meant I grew up on Dungeness crab and Crab Louis, and I put together my own versions long before I left home.

I think a word about Crab Louis is in order here, as it is hard to find a traditional one. According to Jim Sancimino of Swan Oyster Depot, founded in 1912 and the last of dozens of similar places that once thrived in San Francisco, a true Crab Louis consists of just three ingredients: Dungeness crab, crisp iceberg lettuce, and Louis dressing. Everything we add today, from tomatoes, hard-boiled eggs, sliced beets, and avocado to all manner of specialty greens, is a modern conceit. These foods are fine in their own right but they all serve to detract from the main point of the salad: delicious crab napped in voluptuous sauce with crisp lettuce keeping it all bright and refreshing.

Today, I use Louis dressing both traditionally and as others use Thousand Island, with which it shares certain qualities. The signal difference between this and other versions is the whipped cream, which creates a texture that is at once light and voluptuous.

MAKES ABOUT 2 ½ CUPS

½ cup cold heavy cream

½ cup commercial cocktail or chili sauce, such as Heinz or Hunt's

1¼ cups mayonnaise, homemade (page 110) or Best Foods/Hellmann's brand

6 to 8 scallions, white and green parts, trimmed and cut into thin rounds

3 tablespoons minced fresh Italian parsley

Juice of 1 lemon, plus more to taste

1 teaspoon kosher salt, plus more as needed

Black pepper in a mill

Pinch of cayenne pepper or other dried ground chile

RECIPE CONTINUES

Put the cream in a medium bowl (preferably a chilled metal bowl) and use a whisk to whip it until it forms soft peaks.

Use a rubber spatula to gently fold in the cocktail sauce and the mayonnaise, followed by the scallions, parsley, lemon juice, and salt. Do not overmix, or you will decrease the volume of the whipped cream. Season generously with black pepper, add a pinch of cayenne, and mix quickly but gently. Taste, and correct for salt and acid as needed. Use immediately, or refrigerate, covered, for up to 4 days.

BEST USES

Crab Louis; Shrimp Louis; crab and shrimp salad with hard-cooked eggs, roasted beets, roasted asparagus, and lettuce; iceberg wedges; as a dip with crab claws, shrimp, radishes, celery, and carrots; in place of Thousand Island dressing on Reuben sandwiches

GREEN GODDESS DRESSING

File this under "Everything old is new again." For nearly a decade, green goddess dressing has been enjoying a renaissance, and for good reason: It is delicious. My favorite way to make it is with one of the variations that follow the main recipe.

MAKES ABOUT 1½ CUPS

1 cup mayonnaise, homemade (page 110) or Best Foods/Hellmann's
   brand
⅓ cup crème fraîche or sour cream
5 oil-packed anchovy fillets, drained and mashed
2 garlic cloves, minced
3 tablespoons minced fresh Italian parsley
2 tablespoons snipped fresh chives
1 tablespoon minced fresh tarragon
1 teaspoon kosher salt, plus more as needed
2 teaspoons freshly squeezed lemon juice
2 teaspoons white wine vinegar or champagne vinegar

Put the mayonnaise and crème fraîche in a medium bowl and whisk until smooth. Fold in the anchovies, garlic, parsley, chives, and tarragon.

Sprinkle the salt on one area of the dressing, pour the lemon juice and vinegar over it, and agitate the bowl a bit to dissolve the salt. Fold the mixture into the dressing, taste, and correct for salt as needed. Use immediately, or refrigerate, covered, for up to 2 days.

RECIPE CONTINUES

Variations

GREENER GREEN GODDESS DRESSING: Omit the anchovies, chives, and tarragon. Mince $3/4$ cup loosely packed watercress and add it to the dressing along with the parsley.

SORREL GREEN GODDESS DRESSING: Omit the anchovies, chives, and tarragon. Mince $1/2$ cup shredded French sorrel and add it to the dressing along with the parsley.

SPICY LIME GREEN GODDESS DRESSING: Omit the tarragon. Replace the lemon juice with lime juice. Mince $1/2$ cup loosely packed ancho cress, which is very spicy, and 2 tablespoons fresh cilantro and fold into the dressing along with the chives.

BEST USES

Iceberg lettuce wedges topped with rings of red onion; Little Gem lettuces, halved and topped with baby shrimp; avocado halves filled with baby shrimp and cherry tomatoes; grilled cabbage wedges; as a dip with radishes, carrots, celery, jicama, and cherry tomatoes

CHAPTER 4

Sassy *and* Spirited
Salads to Enjoy All Year

"I've never paid attention to salads," a colleague commented as I worked on this book. "I've always thought they were boring," she added, taking another bite of seared scallops and frisée cloaked in walnut vinaigrette.

She gobbled the salad with gusto and was clearly delighted—and not bored!—by what she was eating. A good salad is just that, delightful, and this chapter is meant to fill you with delight, over and over again. Think of the recipes here as templates. Although there are just a dozen or so primary recipes, the seasonal and other variations that follow most of them bring the total to nearly sixty delicious dishes. To these, you will eventually add your own variations, based on inspiration, personal preference, and what is abundant in your garden.

My approach to choosing salad ingredients is simple: I shop first at farmers' markets. Salads always taste best when the ingredients have been harvested in their own time, picked for ripeness and taste and not for durability. Each week during the height of the season, there are 25 markets within easy reach of where I live. If something is available there, that means that it is in season near me. This approach makes seasonal eating simple.

Another benefit of shopping at farmers' markets is that you won't be tempted by all those packaged lettuce leaves, shredded cabbages, whittled carrots—those mature carrots carved by machine to look like baby carrots—and such. These foods are so far past their prime and so inferior to freshly picked heads of lettuce or recently pulled carrots that there is no reason to buy them. Just don't, please.

I can recommend this dish to all who have confidence in me: Salad refreshes without weakening, and comforts without irritating, and I have a habit of saying that it makes us young.

—*The Physiology of Taste*, Jean Anthelme Brillat-Savarin
(translated by M. F. K. Fisher, 1949)

Dressing Up Leafy Greens

Making refreshing, delicious, and healthy green salads is easy, and if you don't have the habit, it is equally easy to adopt it. All it takes is buying the best lettuces you can find or growing the varieties you favor in your garden. When it is time to eat, gather the amount you need, rinse and dry the leaves, put them in a spacious bowl, and dress them lightly, with salt, olive oil or a favorite nut oil, and a bit of acid. Salting the greens before adding the other ingredients keeps the flavors bright—it makes them pop—and you can, if you like, add freshly ground pepper at this time.

This is the basic green salad, simple and delightful. To gussy it up a bit, think outside the bowl, which has been stuck somewhere between about 1963 and the mid 1970s for far too long. Too many salads include out-of-season tomatoes (a legacy of the early '60s); raw vegetables like spinach, broccoli, and mushrooms that really need a bit of cooking (thank you, 1970s health-food fanatics); and gloppy gobs of bottled dressing that weigh everything down and eclipse both flavors and textures. It is high time to move on.

I recommend two approaches to dressing up leafy greens. First, certain ingredients complement and enhance this simple salad, and when you add them sparingly and in compatible combinations, you'll be pleased with the results, as the salad retains its refreshingly ethereal quality.

Second, instead of putting a lot of ingredients into the salad when you want something heartier, put another, more substantial salad on top instead, using the leafy greens as a foundation, a bed. Think of it as "salad on salad," welcome any time of year and ideal on sizzling summer nights and other occasions—after a big holiday feast, for example—when you want to eat lightly. Among my favorite salads to use in this way are crab, mussels, clams, and calamari in Lemon Citronette (page 36); carrots and zucchini steamed separately and tossed individually with Moroccan Melody (page 96); lentils dressed with Richer Ruby Vinaigrette (page 24); chickpea, tuna, and hard-cooked eggs dressed with Parsley Vinaigrette (page 22); and cannellini beans and julienned roasted sweet bell peppers dressed with Not Yo' Mama's Roasted Garlic Vinaigrette (page 31). All potato salads, grain salads, and legume salads can also be served in this way.

I think measuring leafy greens by volume is rather silly, as it makes no sense to stuff greens into a measuring cup. Use your eyes and your hands; I find that about three handfuls make a salad that's perfect for two people. If you feel compelled to measure, get a good digital scale and measure by weight, not volume. Allow 3 ounces of trimmed leafy greens for 3 to 4 people.

Why, you may ask, do I not simply use one of the many dressings in this book for this salad? Although nearly any of them would make a delicious cloak for pert salad greens, this recipe and the variations that follow it are even simpler. The point I want to make here is that a salad at its most basic doesn't even need a quickly made vinaigrette to be deliciously satisfying. That said, there are times when using a dressing is the best option. In such instances, there are two things to keep in mind: First, use a light hand, adding no more than a couple of tablespoons of dressing to a salad for 3 or 4 people. Second, put the dressing in the salad bowl before adding washed, thoroughly dried greens. Use your hands to turn the greens in the dressing gently. With creamy dressings, let the dressing relax in the salad bowl for several minutes before adding the greens; you want it to warm a bit so that it is easier to distribute and doesn't weigh down the lettuce.

SERVES 2

3 large handfuls very fresh leafy salad greens
Kosher salt
Extra-virgin olive oil
Juice of ½ lemon or 1 tablespoon white wine vinegar or
    red wine vinegar
Black pepper in a mill

RECIPE CONTINUES

Put the greens in a wooden bowl, sprinkle lightly with salt, and toss gently. Drizzle with just enough olive oil to coat the leaves lightly; use your hands to turn the leaves gently.

Sprinkle with a little of the lemon juice, turn again, taste, and add more lemon juice until the acid-oil balance pleases you. Season with black pepper and serve immediately.

Variations

GREEN SALAD WITH FRESH HERBS: Add a small handful of fresh herb leaves to the greens before salting them. Any combination of chives, Italian parsley, tarragon, salad burnet, savory, oregano, thyme, and/or mint will enhance the salad, but I don't recommend rosemary, as it will dominate the other flavors.

GREEN SALAD WITH CHEESE CURLS: Use a vegetable peeler to make curls of Parmigiano-Reggiano or aged Monterey Jack and scatter them over the greens before adding the pepper.

GREEN SALAD WITH RADISHES: Cut 3 or 4 radishes into paper-thin slices and add to the greens before salting them.

GREEN SALAD WITH SHALLOTS AND CHEESE: Slice a small shallot into very thin slices and add it to the greens when you salt them. Break 1 to 2 ounces feta cheese or blue cheese into pieces and add to the salad before the pepper. In the spring, try a spring onion instead of a shallot.

GREEN SALAD WITH AVOCADO: Use lime juice as the salad's acid and add half an avocado, cut into very thin lengthwise slices, after adding the oil. A small handful of fresh cilantro is a nice addition, too.

GREEN SALAD WITH WALNUTS AND GOAT CHEESE: Use walnut oil instead of olive oil and sherry vinegar as the acid. After tossing the greens with vinegar, add 2 tablespoons chopped toasted walnuts, 1 to 2 ounces crumbled goat cheese, and 1 tablespoon snipped fresh chives.

GREEN SALAD WITH HAZELNUTS AND POMEGRANATE: Use hazelnut oil instead of olive oil and use pomegranate vinegar, if available, for the acid; if it is not available, use a richly flavored red wine vinegar. After tossing the greens with the vinegar, add about 2 tablespoons chopped toasted hazelnuts, 3 tablespoons fresh pomegranate arils, and about 1 teaspoon grated orange zest.

Insalata Caprese, a classic Italian salad of mozzarella and tomatoes, is tremendously popular in the United States. When tomatoes are in season, it can be deliriously appealing, as good as anything you've ever eaten. Yet too many restaurants and home cooks prepare it year-round, using sad commercial tomatoes with little taste and mealy texture, even though there are better seasonal alternatives. I make classic Caprese only when tomatoes are naturally ripe where I live, but I don't deprive myself at other times. Instead, I use those fruits and vegetables that are at their peak when tomatoes are but a memory. Seasonal variations follow the main recipe.

SERVES 4 TO 6

1 pound fresh mozzarella cheese, preferably *fior di latte* or *mozzarella di bufala*, well chilled

5 to 6 medium-size ripe, backyard-quality tomatoes, preferably a selection of colors, cored

2 to 3 garlic cloves, minced

Kosher salt or Maldon sea salt

⅓ cup best-quality extra-virgin olive oil

12 to 16 medium-size fresh basil leaves

Black pepper in a mill

Sourdough hearth bread

Drain the mozzarella and, if it seems particularly damp, pat it dry with a clean kitchen towel. Set the cheese on a clean work surface and cut into 3/8-inch-thick slices. Set the slices on a plate, cover, and let come to room temperature.

Slice the tomatoes into 1/4-inch-thick rounds, arrange them on a large platter, and scatter the garlic on top. Sprinkle lightly with salt and let rest for 15 to 20 minutes.

To finish the salad, tuck mozzarella slices between the tomatoes and drizzle the olive oil over the tomatoes and cheese. Season with a little more salt.

Working quickly, stack the basil leaves, use a very sharp knife to cut them into thin threads, and scatter them over the salad. Alternatively, do not cut the leaves; instead, tuck them whole between the slices of tomatoes and cheese.

Season with several turns of black pepper and serve, with hot hearth bread alongside.

Variations

PARSLEY AND ONION CAPRESE: Add thinly sliced red onion between the slices of tomato and mozzarella; replace the olive oil with Parsley Vinaigrette (page 22).

CHERRY TOMATO CAPRESE: When you have an abundance of cherry tomatoes, use them to make a wonderful Caprese. To do so, omit the large tomatoes. Remove the stems from about 1 pint of cherry tomatoes, preferably of mixed colors; cut small ones in half and large ones into quarters. Put the tomatoes in a bowl, add the garlic, and season with salt. Let rest for 15 to 20 minutes. To finish the salad, spoon the tomatoes over the cheese on the platter and dress with White Wine Vinaigrette (page 22) or Honey-Pepper Vinaigrette (page 66).

BURRATA CAPRESE: Replace the mozzarella with 2 rounds of burrata. To build the salad, leave room in the center of the platter when you arrange the tomatoes. Add the burrata to the center and break both rounds in half with a soup spoon, so that the interior shards of mozzarella and the cream mingle with the tomato juices. Dress with olive oil or Balsamic Vinaigrette (page 28).

SAVORY FALL CAPRESE: In the urgent season, when the last of the tomatoes are begging to be eaten, I shift from olive oil or a light vinaigrette to Ruby Vinaigrette (page 24), as it echoes the rich, dead-ripe flavors of the season. I also add paper-thin rounds of zucchini, tucking them between the tomatoes and the cheese. If it is available, try using smoked mozzarella in the fall, as it resonates beautifully with ultra-ripe tomatoes.

RECIPE CONTINUES

SWEET FALL CAPRESE: Ripe figs and ripe grapes generally coincide in the fall and make delicious companions. To enjoy them in a Caprese-style salad, cut 6 to 8 figs into quarters lengthwise (grill them first, if you like). Cut 1 medium bunch red grapes in half (you'll need about 1 cup sliced grapes) or, if particularly large, into quarters. Arrange the figs over the room-temperature mozzarella, dress with Balsamic Vinaigrette (page 28) or Walnut Vinaigrette (page 40), scatter the grapes over the top, and add about 2 ounces julienned prosciutto.

WINTER CAPRESE: Several hours or the day before serving the salad, roast 3 or 4 medium beets (a mix of Chioggia, golden, and red, if possible) in a 400°F oven until they are tender when pierced with a bamboo skewer. Remove the beets from the oven and, when they are cool enough to handle, pull off their skins. Refrigerate, covered, until ready to use. To finish the salad, arrange the mozzarella as described in the main recipe. Cut the beets into $1/4$-inch-thick rounds and tuck them between the slices of cheese. Cut 1 large or 2 small avocados into $3/4$-inch cubes and toss with a squeeze of lemon juice to prevent browning. Scatter the avocado over the beets and cheese. Dress with Caraway Vinaigrette (page 38), Walnut Vinaigrette (page 40), Blood Orange Vinaigrette (page 51), or Warm Shallot Vinaigrette (page 71).

SPRING CAPRESE: You'll need about $3/4$ cup shelled, blanched, and peeled fava beans, from 2 to $2^1/2$ pounds unshelled favas. It is helpful to prepare the favas in advance, even the day before. To finish the salad, arrange the mozzarella as described in the main recipe. Cut about 12 fresh young radishes, preferably French breakfast radishes, into thin lengthwise slices. Cut 2 or 3 small spring onions into thin rounds. When the cheese has reached room temperature, scatter the radishes, favas, and onions over it; tuck 8 to 10 very fresh spearmint leaves here and there and scatter 2 tablespoons minced fresh chives on top.

Season with salt and dress with either extra-virgin olive oil, White Wine Vinaigrette (page 22), or Not Yo' Mama's Roasted Garlic Vinaigrette (page 31).

PASTA CAPRESE: To turn any of these versions of a Caprese into a delicious pasta salad, cook 5 or 6 ounces of cencioni—literally, "little rags"—according to package directions. When the pasta is al dente, drain and rinse it and shake off as much water as possible. Drizzle a little olive oil on a serving platter, arrange the cencioni atop the oil, season the pasta lightly with salt and pepper, and build the salad on top of it, so that the ingredients and dressing flavor the pasta.

Every August, friends and colleagues host a benefit for the Sonoma County Book Festival at Windrush Farm in Petaluma, a beautifully rustic working farm operated by Mimi Luebbermann, who also writes cookbooks. Several years ago, J.J. Wilson—Mimi's sister, one of the festival's founders and a dear friend—asked if I had a recipe for a good salad she could make for the benefit. I suggested this one, which I developed shortly after the century-long ban on absinthe in America was lifted in 2007. The salad was so popular that J.J. now must make it every year. Not that she minds; she loves it as much as we all do and as you will, once you've tried it. Be sure to save the juices that collect on the platter; we like to tip them into our wine glasses for a post-party cocktail.

SERVES 6 TO 8

1 medium-size ripe honeydew or other green-fleshed muskmelon, halved and seeded
4 to 5 medium-size lemon cucumbers, peeled and thinly sliced
1 recipe Mina's Tears (page 85)
Handful of fresh spearmint leaves, for garnish

Cut the melon into 2-inch cubes, removing all the skin and any tough rind.

Scatter the cubed melon over a large platter or wide shallow bowl, tuck the cucumber slices here and there, and pour over the dressing. Gently turn the melon and cucumbers to be sure they've been napped with the dressing. Cover and refrigerate for at least 30 minutes and as long as 3 hours before serving.

Garnish with the spearmint leaves and serve cold.

Slaw!

Call it coleslaw, vegetable slaw, cabbage salad, or whatever you like, it's a culinary workhorse, found in delis, fish-and-chips cafés, all manner of ethnic eateries, and even high-end restaurants. In the Carolinas, coleslaw is piled directly on top of pulled pork sandwiches, and Salvadoran pupusas are typically accompanied by curtido, a lightly fermented cabbage salad.

Lately, I've come to think of slaw as a miracle. It's an amazingly efficient and delicious way both to eat a wide variety of vegetables and to deal with the abundance of a productive vegetable garden. I usually make some sort of slaw every Sunday, as produce from the several farmers' markets I attend each week begs for attention. My grandson Lucas, who is 10, cannot get enough of it, no matter the time of year; he even loves it in the winter, when it includes raw Brussels sprouts.

I find that texture is as important as taste in a slaw and recommend using the thinnest slicing blade of a good food processor for most of the ingredients. It's fast and the results are outstanding, as a uniform texture is pleasing to our palates in much the same way certain repeating patterns are pleasing to our eyes. I confess I am a bit of a math geek and a great admirer of Fibonacci, the nickname

of Leonardo Pisano Bigollo, the 12th-century mathematician from Pisa who was one of the first to observe and codify certain repeating patterns found in nature that are today referred to as Fibonacci numbers, the Fibonacci sequence, and the Golden Ratio. We perceive these patterns as beautiful, and I believe we grasp this through the sense of touch as well as visually. But I digress.

Coleslaw should reflect the vegetables in season at the time it is made; if there are no carrots in season, for example, simply omit them. You can add radishes whenever they are available. Celery, too, is an excellent addition, as long as it is sliced as thin as the other ingredients.

One word of advice: Certain regional coleslaw recipes call for apples, canned pineapple, or mandarin oranges. Although these additions may be traditional, I urge caution. I make apple coleslaw in the fall, during the local apple harvest, and prepare just enough to enjoy immediately, as the apples break down and darken when the salad is refrigerated. Canned pineapple and mandarin oranges are cloyingly sweet and eclipse more subtle flavors in the slaw; I do not recommend them.

This main recipe, as close to traditional coleslaw as I get, is followed by seasonal variations.

SERVES 6 TO 8

1 small head white cabbage, or ½ small head red cabbage and ½ small
   head white cabbage
1 small red onion, trimmed and peeled
2 medium-size carrots, trimmed and peeled
½ cup chopped fresh Italian parsley
3 tablespoons red wine vinegar
3 tablespoons sugar
Kosher salt
Black pepper in a mill
Tabasco or other hot pepper sauce
2 tablespoons ground cumin
¾ cup mayonnaise, homemade (page 110) or Best Foods/
   Hellmann's brand
½ cup crème fraîche
2 tablespoons Dijon mustard

Cut the cabbage into quarters, slicing lengthwise through the poles, not crosswise through the equator. Cut out the core and then cut the cabbage into lengthwise wedges that will fit through your food processor's largest feed tube. Cut the onion into wedges that will fit, as well.

Using the processor's thinnest slicing blade, slice the cabbage and onion, transferring the sliced vegetables to a large bowl whenever the processor's work bowl is nearly full. Switch to a large grating blade and grate the carrots. If you prefer, you may use a very sharp chef's knife to cut the cabbage and onion into very thin ribbons and the large blade of a box grater to grate the carrots. Add the grated carrots and the chopped parsley to the cabbage and onions and toss well.

Put the red wine vinegar and sugar in a medium bowl and stir to dissolve the sugar. Season generously with kosher salt, several turns of black pepper, and a few shakes of Tabasco. Add the cumin, whisk a time or two, and fold in the mayonnaise, crème fraîche, and mustard. Taste, and correct for salt and pepper as needed. Pour the dressing over the vegetables and toss well.

Serve immediately or refrigerate, covered, for up to 4 days. Always stir it well before serving.

Variations

SPRING SLAW: Use about half the amount of cabbage called for in the main recipe. Add about 3 cups thinly shredded arugula, 10 to 12 thinly sliced radishes, and 1 very thinly sliced fennel bulb; all these vegetables may be put through a food processor fitted with the thinnest slicing blade. Instead of the dressing called for in the main recipe, use 1 1/4 cups Creamy Sesame-Ginger Dressing (page 115). Add 3 tablespoons chopped fresh cilantro after adding the dressing. For a lighter coleslaw, omit the creamy dressing and use Ginger-Mustard Vinaigrette (page 63) instead, along with the chopped cilantro.

EARLY SUMMER SLAW: When blueberries are in season, add about 1 1/2 cups to the classic coleslaw and use blueberry vinegar, if available, in place of the red wine vinegar. Omit the cumin and add 1/2 teaspoon ground cloves. Grate 1 medium kohlrabi using the large blade of a box grater or the grating blade of a food processor and toss it with the fruit and vegetables before adding the dressing. Cut 12 to 16 basil leaves into very thin julienne and add to the slaw after adding the dressing.

RECIPE CONTINUES

FALL SLAW: Raspberries are often at their sweetest in the fall, when September's heat coaxes their sugars to rise. To make raspberry coleslaw, use 2 tablespoons raspberry or hibiscus vinegar and 1 tablespoon freshly squeezed lemon juice instead of the red wine vinegar. Omit the carrot and add a pint of fresh raspberries to the vegetables.

WINTER SLAW: Cabbage is at its peak in the winter, as it benefits from cold weather. The same is true for other brassicas, such as Brussels sprouts, which can be used raw in coleslaw provided they are sliced very thinly. Other seasonal options include parsnips, grated as carrots are grated; very thinly sliced kale; and shaved rutabaga. Dress as described in the main recipe or with Green Goddess Dressing (page 129).

The Best Potato Salads

The world is full of delicious potato salads, from simple mixtures of potatoes, onions, and mayonnaise to complex combinations that include everything from celery, olives, cucumbers, pickles, and eggs to carrots, parsnips, fava beans, peas, radishes, beets, horseradish, tomatoes, chiles, mushrooms, green beans, goat cheese, blue cheese, anchovies, sardines, smoked salmon, sausage, bacon, macaroni, all manner of herbs, and even premium ingredients like crab, lobster, and fresh truffles. In communities around the country, there are countless examples of the "best potato salad in the world," dishes that must be part of church picnics, neighborhood potlucks, and other special events. Certain regions like their potato salads at least a little bit sweet, something that is usually accomplished with the addition of sweet pickle relish or a commercial dressing such as Miracle Whip; in other regions, savory is the rule.

When I was a very young cook, still in my mid teens, I learned that the best way to make an irresistible potato salad is to marinate the still-warm potatoes in some sort of vinaigrette or, in certain instances, bacon fat. All these many years later, this technique never lets me down. I vary the marinade depending on the final results I want and what will be served alongside, but I always marinate the potatoes while they are as warm as possible, as heat facilitates the absorption of the marinade.

The single exception is when I make potato salad for a luau. Although there are variations—each with its own champions—I believe Hawaiian potato salad should consist of diced potatoes, diced white onions, diced celery, chopped California black olives, quartered hard-cooked eggs, Best Foods mayonnaise, salt, and black pepper. Now and then I'll add elbow macaroni for potato-mac salad, also a traditional luau dish. That's it, nothing more.

This salad, inspired by the warm potato salads—*pommes à l'huile*—of France, is extraordinary just as it is, especially if you use flavorful dry-farmed potatoes, often available at farmers' markets. It also makes an excellent building block for more complex salads, as suggested in the variations that follow the main recipe.

SERVES 4 TO 6

2 pounds small new potatoes, peeled and cut into ⅜-inch-thick slices

⅔ cup White Wine Vinaigrette (page 22), Not Yo' Mama's Roasted
    Garlic Vinaigrette (page 31), Caraway Vinaigrette (page 38), or
    Warm Shallot Vinaigrette (page 71)

2 tablespoons white wine

¾ cup loosely packed fresh Italian parsley, chopped

2 tablespoons snipped fresh chives

Kosher salt

Black pepper in a mill

Put the sliced potatoes in the basket of a steamer set over boiling water and cook until tender but not mushy or falling apart, about 18 minutes.

While the potatoes steam, divide the vinaigrette in half, putting half in one small bowl and half in another. Add the white wine to one bowl.

When the potatoes are tender, put them in a medium bowl, drizzle the vinaigrette-wine mixture over them, and toss very gently. Set aside for 20 to 30 minutes to allow the potatoes to absorb the dressing.

To finish the salad, toss the potatoes with the other half of the dressing, half of the parsley, and half of the chives. Season with salt and several turns of black pepper.

RECIPE CONTINUES

Toss and transfer to a serving bowl or platter. Sprinkle with the remaining parsley and chives and serve warm immediately, refrigerate for up to 3 days, or use as a base for a more complex salad.

Variations

CREAMY POTATO SALAD: Marinate the salad as directed in the main recipe, but omit the white wine from the marinade. Omit the remaining vinaigrette and parsley. Add 2 quartered or sliced hard-cooked eggs, 3 or 4 celery stalks cut into small dice, and a handful of very thinly sliced radishes to the potatoes after they've rested in the marinade for 30 minutes. Dress with Mustard Mayonnaise (page 110) and fold into the salad.

RUSSIAN EGG POTATO SALAD: Marinate the warm potatoes in $1/2$ cup Caraway Vinaigrette (page 38). After letting the potatoes rest for about 30 minutes, add 2 carrots that have been peeled, diced and steamed; 1 medium beet, peeled, diced, and steamed; 6 or 7 green onions, trimmed and thinly sliced; and 1 cup blanched fresh English peas. Dress with all but 2 tablespoons of a batch of Mustard Mayonnaise (page 110) and top the salad with 6 hard-cooked eggs, cut in half lengthwise. Top each half egg with a dollop of the remaining Mustard Mayonnaise and, if you like, a little spoonful of black caviar.

POTATO SALAD WITH BACON AND TOMATOES: Marinate the warm potatoes in Savory Bacon Vinaigrette (page 79). Fold in 2 cups of quartered cherry tomatoes and top with 3 or 4 strips of bacon that have been cooked until crisp and then crumbled.

GREEN BEAN AND POTATO SALAD: When green beans come into season, add some to the salad. To do so, cut about 1 pound Blue Lakes, Romanos, Spanish Musica, or other green beans into $1^1/2$-inch lengths (leave haricots verts whole), cook in boiling salted water until just tender, drain, cool slightly, and fold into the potatoes after they have been marinated. Finish with Cherry Tomato Vinaigrette (page 46) and replace the parsley and chives with fresh basil. This version is also quite good with thinly sliced radishes.

LAMB TONGUE SALAD: Lamb tongue, once a popular ingredient in America, is making a comeback as an increasingly conscientious public understands that using all parts of an animal is the best sustainable practice. To make this salad, which is among my all-time favorites, simply poach 7 or 8 lamb tongues in salted water for about 45 minutes or until they are quite tender when pierced with the tip of a paring knife. Let the tongues sit in the poaching liquid until they are just cool enough to handle, and then peel the skins off while they are still warm. Cut into 1/4-inch-thick diagonal slices, arrange on top of the salad before adding the second half of the dressing, top with that dressing and the herbs, and serve warm. The White Wine Vinaigrette is ideally suited to the lamb's tongue, but if you like, Savory Bacon Vinaigrette (page 79) or Italian-Style Salsa Verde (page 90) could make a fun and delicious alternative.

WARM SWEET POTATO SALAD: Peel, cut, and steam 2 pounds sweet potatoes as described in the main recipe and marinate them in a mixture of 3 tablespoons olive oil, 1 tablespoon sherry vinegar, 1 tablespoon warmed molasses, salt, and black pepper for 30 minutes. Add 3/4 cup lightly toasted shelled pecans, 1 minced shallot, and 3 tablespoons chopped Italian parsley, and dress with Warm Bacon-Maple Vinaigrette (page 77) or Honey-Pepper Vinaigrette (page 66).

My Take on Pasta Salad

Pasta salad can be tricky to make successfully. Too often, pasta salads are made with sturdy shapes—fusilli, for example, or penne—that are really best served hot with a hearty sauce. Many pasta salads are also made in the style of potato salad, with a mayonnaise-based dressing and large chunks of undercooked vegetables. My preferences are elsewhere.

In pasta salads, I often like to combine a small pasta—rosamarina (also known as orzo), acini di pepe, or another small seed-size soup pasta—with other grains or legumes and dress the mixture at the last minute with a simple vinaigrette. Chickpeas, lentils, and farro all work well with pasta in this way. In the spring I include fresh favas, and in the summer, I add quartered cherry tomatoes. Sometimes I add good canned tuna, crumbled feta cheese, sliced hard-cooked egg, and celery cut into

small dice. Dressed in a light, tangy vinaigrette, salads such as these are refreshing, delicious, and not at all heavy. When there is leftover pasta salad, it should, of course, be refrigerated, but it must be allowed to return to room temperature before serving, so that the dressing relaxes and the flavors wake up.

Strand pasta—from linguini to Southeast Asian rice noodles and Japanese buckwheat noodles—makes a good salad, too. One of my favorite versions is simply classic Caesar salad tossed with room temperature spaghettini. Vietnamese bun, which combines rice vermicelli with shredded lettuce, julienned carrots, mung beans, barbecued pork or other meat or seafood, and a sweet-hot dressing, is one of the world's greatest noodle salads, deserving of its own book.

SERVES 6 TO 8

1 pound small lumache (snail-shaped), gigli (cone-shaped), or torchio
    (torch-shaped) pasta

Kosher salt

1 recipe Not Yo' Mama's Roasted Garlic Vinaigrette (page 31)

8 ounces small cleaned squid, tentacles and bodies separated

1 tablespoon olive oil

¾ cup freshly steamed and shelled Manila clams (see Note page 154)

¾ cup freshly steamed and shelled mussels (see Note page 154)

¾ cup fresh crabmeat, preferably Dungeness, picked over

¾ cup cooked baby shrimp, preferably wild

2 lemons, 1 halved and 1 cut into wedges

3 tablespoons chopped fresh Italian parsley

Black pepper in a mill

Fill a large pot two-thirds full with water, add a very generous tablespoon of salt, and bring the water to a boil over high heat. Add the pasta and stir with a wooden spoon until the water returns to a boil. Cook according to package directions until the pasta is just done. Drain, rinse in cool water, drain thoroughly, and transfer to a wide, shallow bowl. Pour about half of the vinaigrette over the pasta and toss gently. Set aside.

Meanwhile, cut the squid bodies into ¼-inch rounds. Pour the olive oil into a medium sauté pan set over medium-high heat, add the squid bodies and tentacles, and sauté, turning or tossing nearly continuously, until the squid just loses its raw look, about 2 minutes. Season with salt and remove from the heat.

RECIPE CONTINUES

Put the squid, clams, mussels, crabmeat, and shrimp in a bowl, squeeze the juice of the lemon halves over the seafood, toss, and season with salt and several turns of black pepper. Cover and refrigerate for 1 hour.

To finish the salad, add the shellfish to the pasta, along with the remaining vinaigrette and the parsley. Toss very gently, taste, and correct for salt and pepper as needed. Garnish with lemon wedges and serve immediately.

Note: It takes about 1 pound of Manila clams and 1 pound of mussels to yield $3/4$ cup each of shellfish meat. To steam the shellfish, pour about $1/4$ inch of white wine into a large pot, add a big squeeze of lemon juice, and add the clams and mussels. Set over high heat and when the liquid begins to boil, cover and cook until the shells open, which usually takes about 3 minutes but can take as long as 5 or 6. Remove from the heat, cool slightly, and discard any shellfish that remain fully shut. Pick the meat from the shells.

Variations

Use Creamy Lemon Citronette (page 34), Lime-Cayenne Citronette (page 37), or Warm Shallot Vinaigrette (page 71) instead of the garlic vinaigrette.

This salad is beautiful to behold, with cranberries and pomegranates shimmering like little jewels. To accent the visual elements, use all jasmine rice instead of a blend of jasmine and wild rices. If you happen to have a couple cups of cherry tomatoes, slice them into quarters and add them to the salad along with the onion, pomegranate arils, and cranberries. You can follow this basic formula—3 1/2 cups cooked rice, 1 cup of dressing, and about 1 1/2 cups of other similar-size ingredients—to make rice salads throughout the year.

SERVES 6

2 cups cooked jasmine rice (from about ⅔ cup raw rice), cooled and
    fluffed with a fork
1½ cups cooked wild rice (from about ½ cup raw rice), cooled
    and fluffed with a fork
Juice of 1 lemon
Kosher salt
Black pepper in a mill
1 cup Persephone's Pleasure (page 58)
1 small red onion, cut into small dice
¾ cup fresh pomegranate arils (from 1 large pomegranate)
⅓ cup minced fresh cranberries
Zest of 1 orange
3 tablespoons minced fresh Italian parsley
2 tablespoons snipped fresh chives
3 tablespoons walnut halves, lightly toasted and chopped, or lightly
    toasted pine nuts (see Note page 156)
8 to 10 large lettuce leaves

RECIPE CONTINUES

Put the rice and wild rice in a large bowl, drizzle with the lemon juice, season with salt and pepper, and toss. Let rest for 10 to 15 minutes.

Add half the vinaigrette along with the onion, all but 2 tablespoons of the pomegranate arils, the cranberries, and orange zest and toss thoroughly. Add the parsley, chives, and walnuts and toss again.

Arrange the lettuce leaves on a platter or in a bowl and spoon the salad on top of it. Alternatively, arrange on individual salad plates. Drizzle with the remaining dressing and serve.

Note: I recommend using only domestic, European, or Korean pine nuts, which are, alas, both hard to find and expensive, as nearly all readily available pine nuts now come from China. A few years ago, some individuals in the United States began experiencing a persistent bitter taste in the mouth lasting for days, weeks, or months. The condition, known colloquially as "pine mouth," has been traced to the consumption of pine nuts. Early investigations suggest the culprit may be a variety of Chinese pine nut that triggers the response in some people. For this reason, and because I developed pine mouth shortly after eating Chinese pine nuts and found it an unpleasant and disturbing experience, I recommend avoiding pine nuts from China unless you know you are not sensitive to them.

Variations

SPRING SALADE BIJOU: Omit the pomegranate arils, cranberries, orange zest, and walnuts. Use comparable quantities of blanched English peas, roasted asparagus cut in 1-inch diagonal slices, and lightly toasted pistachios. Dress with Warm Fava Vinaigrette (page 75).

SUMMER SALADE BIJOU: Omit the pomegranate arils, cranberries, orange zest, walnuts, and chives. Cut 2 cups cherry tomatoes (preferably of various colors) into quarters and toss with the rice, along with toasted pine nuts and a small handful of fresh basil leaves, shredded. Dress with Ruby Vinaigrette (page 24), Italian-Style Salsa Verde (page 90), or Moroccan Melody (page 96).

SPICY SUMMER SALADE BIJOU: Omit the wild rice, pomegranate arils, cranberries, orange zest, walnuts, and chives. Add 1 cup cooked black beans; 1 cup fresh corn kernels, just cut from the cob; 2 roasted, peeled, and julienned poblano chiles; and 1 or 2 minced serrano chiles. Dress with Lime Citronette (page 36) or Lime-Cayenne Citronette (page 37).

WINTER SALADE BIJOU: Omit the pomegranate arils, cranberries, and chives. Add 2 cups diced roasted beets—preferably a mix of white, golden, Chioggia, and red—and dress with Not Yo' Mama's Roasted Garlic Vinaigrette (page 31), Apple Cider Vinaigrette (page 52), or Zinfandel Vinaigrette (page 43).

Two Bread Salads

A recipe for bread salad really should be an idea or concept and not a formula. But we live in an era of recipes, and so here I present two of my favorites, with variations and abundant encouragement for you to embrace the concept and develop your own. There are just a few simple principles involved in making excellent bread salad. First, you need good bread, preferably sturdy hearth bread that won't disintegrate when a vinaigrette is added to moisten and flavor it. Second, other ingredients should be seasonal, preferably at their peak of ripeness. Finally, let the salad rest after dressing it so that the bread absorbs the dressing and the flavors meld.

"Panzanella" is simply the Italian name for bread salad, and it has taken its place in the English language as have so many other Italian culinary terms.

SERVES 4 TO 6

4 ripe heirloom tomatoes, cored and chopped
3 to 4 garlic cloves, minced
1 small sweet onion, cut into small dice
Kosher salt
Juice of 1 lemon or 2 tablespoons best-quality wine vinegar, plus
    more as needed
½ cup extra-virgin olive oil, plus more as needed
3 cups cubed rustic hearth bread, about 2 days old
¾ cup loosely packed fresh basil
3 tablespoons chopped fresh Italian parsley
Black pepper in a mill

Put the tomatoes, garlic, and onion in a medium bowl, season with salt, and toss gently. Add the lemon juice and half the olive oil and toss again. Add the bread and several turns of black pepper, and toss again. Cover and let rest for about 30 minutes.

Taste a piece of the bread to see how much liquid it has absorbed. If it seems dry and hard, add the remaining olive oil, toss again, and let rest for 15 minutes more.

Meanwhile, tear the basil leaves into smallish pieces. Add the basil and parsley to the salad, season with several turns of black pepper, and toss. Taste, and correct for salt, pepper, and acid as needed.

Serve at room temperature. The salad can be refrigerated, covered, for up to 2 days but should be removed from the refrigerator 30 minutes before serving.

RECIPE CONTINUES

Variations

AVOCADO PANZANELLA: Omit the sweet onion and basil. Cut 1 medium or 2 small firm-ripe Hass avocados into $1/2$-inch cubes and add to the tomatoes, along with 5 trimmed and very thinly sliced scallions and 2 minced serrano chiles. Replace the basil with $1/2$ cup fresh cilantro leaves, chopped. This version is also excellent with the Lime-Cayenne Citronette (page 37) in place of the lemon juice and oil.

BLT IN A BOWL: Fry 3 or 4 slices of good bacon until crisp. Drain, crumble, and toss them with the bread and tomatoes. Omit the basil and serve the salad on a bed of shredded lettuce and drizzle with squiggles of mayonnaise. *Voilà!* It's a BLT Bread Salad. Alternatively, dress the salad with Savory Bacon Vinaigrette (page 79) instead of the lemon juice and oil.

BREAD SALAD WITH CRUNCH: Add 1 cup thinly sliced cucumbers and 1 cup very thinly sliced celery stalks.

MEDITERRANEAN BREAD SALAD: Add 1 cup roasted and julienned sweet peppers, 2 teaspoons minced garlic, and 8 ounces fresh mozzarella cheese, torn into shards. Dress with Ruby Vinaigrette (page 24) instead of the lemon juice and oil.

GREEN PEPPERCORN AND OLIVE BREAD SALAD: Add $1/2$ cup pitted green olives, cut in half; 2 to 3 small julienned zucchini; and 2 teaspoons brined green peppercorns. Dress with Caper Vinaigrette (page 23) instead of the lemon juice and oil.

BREAD SALAD WITH SAUSAGE: Fry 2 or 3 sausages of your choice, cut them into $1/4$-inch-thick slices on the diagonal, and add them to the salad. Dress with Simple Mustard Vinaigrette (page 23) instead of the lemon juice and oil.

Make this salad in the fall, when harvest is in its final frenzy, and feel free to vary the ingredients based on what is ripe near you. Use nectarines in place of peaches or pears, add a handful of sautéed grapes, or use diced tomatoes instead of cherry tomatoes. I like to serve this salad mounded on top of leaves of butter lettuce, with roasted chicken alongside.

SERVES 4 TO 6

2 shallots, minced
2 teaspoons sugar
1 recipe Apple Cider Vinaigrette (page 52)
1 (1-pound) loaf sourdough hearth bread, preferably a day old
Olive oil
2 tablespoons butter
2 ripe white peaches or firm-ripe pears
¾ cup pitted black olives of your choice, halved
1 cup cherry tomatoes, quartered
2 teaspoons fresh thyme
3 tablespoon minced fresh Italian parsley
Kosher salt
Black pepper in a mill

Put the shallot in a small bowl, add the sugar and the vinaigrette, stir, and set aside.

To prepare the bread, preheat the oven broiler and cut the loaf in half crosswise. Stand one piece, cut side down, on a work surface and use a sharp bread knife to remove the crusts. Trim the second piece similarly. Discard the crusts or save them to make bread crumbs.

RECIPE CONTINUES

Brush the bread all over with just a little olive oil and set under the broiler; turn it several times until all surfaces have been lightly toasted. Let the bread cool, then tear it into 2-inch pieces and put the torn bread in a large bowl. You'll need 4$\frac{1}{2}$ to 5 cups for the salad; if there is more, reserve it for another use, such as making croutons.

Melt the butter in a medium sauté pan. Working quickly, cut the peaches, if using, into medium wedges. If using pears, quickly peel and core them and cut them into $3/4$-inch dice. Sauté the fruit, turning it gently with a metal spatula, until it is lightly browned all over.

Remove from the heat and add to the bowl with the bread, along with the olives, cherry tomatoes, thyme, and parsley. Toss very gently, add the vinaigrette, and toss again. Cover and let rest for 15 minutes.

Taste, and correct for salt and pepper as needed. The salad is best served immediately.

Traditional Lebanese tabbouleh is unlike what comes to mind for most Americans when they think of this popular grain-based salad. In Lebanon, cracked wheat or bulgur is a minor ingredient, more like a garnish that is tossed with a lot of flat-leaf (Italian) parsley and mint, along with bits of tomato and thin slices of scallion, napped in lemon juice and olive oil spiked with cinnamon, allspice, and black pepper. My version, which I make only when there are local tomatoes, has evolved over the years from one that is typically American to one that is more my own. If you like things on the spicy side, add the serranos; otherwise, omit them. On hot summer nights, I add a generous wedge of feta cheese alongside and call it dinner.

SERVES 6 TO 8

1 cup medium-grain bulgur

1 recipe Lemon Citronette (page 36)

1 or 2 serrano chiles, minced (optional)

1 bunch (8 to 10) scallions, trimmed and thinly sliced

1 cucumber, peeled, seeded, and minced

4 medium-size backyard-quality tomatoes, preferably heirloom, cut into
    small dice

¾ cup minced fresh Italian parsley

½ cup minced fresh cilantro

½ cup fresh mint, shredded

Kosher salt

Black pepper in a mill

Put the bulgur in a strainer, shake out any debris, rinse under cool water, and set the strainer with the grain in it in a large bowl. Cover with water and set aside for 10 minutes.

RECIPE CONTINUES

Drain off the water, wrap the bulgur in a clean kitchen towel, and twist to squeeze out excess moisture. Put the bulgur in a large, wide glass or ceramic bowl and pour the dressing over it.

Scatter the serranos, if using, and the scallions over the surface of the bulgur and top with the cucumber. Spread the diced tomatoes on top of the cucumber. Toss the parsley, cilantro, and mint together and spread the mixture evenly over the tomatoes. Cover tightly with plastic wrap and refrigerate for several hours or overnight.

To serve, use two large salad spoons or forks to toss the ingredients together, being sure to reach to the bottom of the bowl to incorporate the bulgur and dressing. Taste, and correct for salt and pepper as needed. Serve immediately, or refrigerate, covered, for up to 3 days. Serve cold or at room temperature.

Because I love tabbouleh and don't want to be without it when tomatoes are not in season, I developed this version. I was inspired by the sorrel that grows so well in my garden, especially in winter and spring, when there are also excellent avocados at local farmers' markets. If you don't have sorrel, use arugula, especially the smaller variety that is often identified as "wild" at farmers' markets. Although arugula is available year-round these days, it is best when grown in cold weather, when it has both its characteristic bitterness and a refreshing snap. If you have neither sorrel nor arugula, use fresh spinach.

SERVES 6 TO 8

1 cup medium-grain bulgur
Generous pinch of ground cinnamon
1 recipe Lime-Cayenne Citronette (page 37)
1 bunch (8 to 10) scallions, trimmed and thinly sliced
½ cup minced fresh Italian parsley
½ cup minced fresh cilantro
½ cup fresh mint, shredded
2 cups fresh sorrel leaves, cut in very thin slices, or 2 cups small arugula
    leaves, or 2 cups young spinach leaves, chopped
2 firm-ripe avocados, diced and tossed with lime juice
Kosher salt
Black pepper in a mill

Place the bulgur in a strainer or colander, shake out any debris, rinse under cool water, and set the strainer with the grain in it in a large bowl. Cover with water and set aside for 10 minutes.

RECIPE CONTINUES

Drain off the water, wrap the bulgur in a clean kitchen towel, and twist to squeeze out excess moisture. While the bulgur soaks, add the pinch of cinnamon to the dressing and set aside briefly.

Put the bulgur in a large, wide glass or ceramic bowl and pour the dressing over it. Scatter the scallions over the surface of the bulgur; add the parsley, cilantro, and mint, and end with the sorrel. Top with the avocados, cover tightly with plastic wrap, and refrigerate for several hours before serving.

To serve, use two large salad spoons or forks to toss the ingredients together, being sure to reach to the bottom of the bowl to incorporate the bulgur and its dressing. Taste, and correct for salt and pepper as needed. Serve immediately, or refrigerate, covered, for up to 3 days. Serve cold or at room temperature.

Farro is my favorite of the many sturdy grains that work so well in salads. I love both its toothsome texture and its earthy flavor and find it needs nothing more than a bright vinaigrette and a few herbs, though it welcomes additions, too. Other grains can be prepared in the same way with a similarly delicious outcome. Couscous, quinoa, lentils, black forbidden rice, chickpeas, and barley, which should be toasted first, all blossom with this technique. I sometimes vary the dressing as well, pairing couscous with Moroccan Melody (page 96), for example, and quinoa with Argentine Elixir (page 88). Relax, have fun, and discover your own favorite combinations.

SERVES 6 TO 8

1 cup semipearled farro, rinsed
Kosher salt
Juice of 1 lemon
1 recipe Lemon Citronette (page 36)
3 or 4 scallions, trimmed and very thinly sliced
Generous handful of fresh Italian parsley, chopped
Small handful of fresh cilantro, chopped (optional)

Put the farro in a medium saucepan, cover with water by 2 inches, season generously with salt, and bring to a boil over high heat. Reduce the heat to low and simmer gently until the farro is tender but still has a bit of chew, 35 to 40 minutes. Let cool for 10 minutes or so, and then drain.

Transfer the drained farro to a wide, shallow mixing bowl, sprinkle the lemon juice over it, toss, and let rest for 15 to 20 minutes.

Add the dressing, scallions, parsley, and cilantro, if using. Toss, taste, and correct for salt as needed. Serve immediately, at room temperature, or refrigerate for up to 2 days; let the salad return to room temperature before serving.

Variations

SPRING FARRO SALAD: Add 2 cups shelled, blanched, and peeled fava beans or 2 cups shelled and blanched English peas, along with 6 ounces crumbled feta cheese. If you like, substitute Warm Fava Vinaigrette (page 75) for the Lemon Citronette.

SUMMER FARRO SALAD: Add 2 cups quartered cherry tomatoes and 1 cup diced zucchini. Omit the cilantro and use about 3 tablespoons finely shredded fresh basil.

FALL FARRO SALAD: Add 2 cups cooked chickpeas, 1 cup diced and steamed carrots, and 1 cup diced and lightly steamed zucchini. Dress with Moroccan Melody (page 96).

WINTER FARRO SALAD: Add 2 cups cooked lentils and about 4 ounces ricotta salata cheese, grated on a large blade. Dress with Richer Ruby Vinaigrette (page 24).

Southeast Asian salads are among the most delicious in the world. I could eat Vietnamese bun—made with rice vermicelli, shredded lettuce, cucumber, carrot, and, sometimes, mung bean sprouts, topped with pork, beef, or seafood and a simple sweet-hot dressing—daily for weeks without growing tired of it. Green papaya salad, with refreshing unripe papaya shaved into noodle-like threads and tossed with long beans, tomatoes, and a tangy dressing, is equally enchanting, and I make it at home when my local Asian market has green papayas. But my favorite salad of this region is Thai larb or laab, in its many variations. Most often it is made of either ground pork or chicken seasoned with garlic, galangal, and toasted rice powder, served over shredded cabbage and dressed with that classic combination of lime juice, fish sauce, sugar, garlic, and hot green chiles. I've had similar salads made with ground beef, ground turkey, minced duck, tiny calamari, and baby octopus, and I've enjoyed these various interpretations atop rice noodles, yam noodles, and salad greens. In this version, which I make from fall to mid spring, I call for spaghetti squash instead of noodles. Spaghetti squash is delicious, healthful, and easy to work with, as it pretty much shreds itself into noodle-like strands after it's cooked. To make this salad with cabbage or rice noodles, consult the variations.

SERVES 4

1 shallot, peeled and chopped

3 garlic cloves, peeled and crushed

1 (1-inch) piece fresh ginger, peeled and chopped

1 serrano chile, stemmed and chopped

Kosher salt

1 pound grass-fed lamb, pork, or beef or pastured duck
   or chicken, ground

2 tablespoons toasted ground rice (see Note below)

6 cups cooked and shredded spaghetti squash, from a 2½- to
    3-pound squash (see Note page 172; can be made several
    hours ahead)

1 recipe Thai Lime Dressing (page 84)

2 or 3 scallions, trimmed and cut into thin rounds

⅓ cup fresh cilantro, torn into pieces

10 to 12 spearmint leaves, torn into pieces

2 teaspoons lightly toasted white sesame seeds or 2 tablespoons
    roasted peanuts (optional)

Put the shallot, garlic, ginger, and serrano in a suribachi (see page 12) or large mortar, season with several pinches of salt, and pound into a paste with a wooden pestle.

Set a medium sauté pan over medium-high heat, add the ground meat, and sauté for 2 to 3 minutes, until it just begins to firm up. Add the shallot paste. Continue to cook, stirring continuously with a fork, for another 4 to 5 minutes, until the meat is no longer pink. Stir in the ground rice and remove from the heat.

To serve, divide the spaghetti squash among four individual soup plates and spoon the meat and cooking juices over each portion. Drizzle the dressing on top, using all of it. Scatter the scallions, cilantro, spearmint, and sesame seeds, if using, over each portion and serve immediately.

Note: Though toasted ground rice is available in Asian markets, it's very easy to make at home. Put ½ cup uncooked rice in a heavy pan—cast iron is ideal—and set over high heat. Stir constantly, preferably with a wooden spoon, until the rice turns golden brown; do not let it burn. Tip into a bowl to cool and then grind to a powder in a spice grinder or coffee grinder used only for spices. Store in a jar or other airtight container.

RECIPE CONTINUES

Note: The easiest way to prepare spaghetti squash is to steam it. If you cut it in half lengthwise and then cut each half into 2 or 3 lengthwise wedges, it will cook fairly quickly, in about 12 minutes. Simply put it on a rack or in the basket of a steamer set over simmering water, cover, and cook until tender but not mushy. If you prefer to bake it, cut it in half lengthwise, cut each half lengthwise in half, set on a baking sheet, and bake at 375°F until tender but not mushy, 20 to 25 minutes. With either cooking method, set the cooked squash aside until cool enough to handle, then scrape out the seeds and use a fork to scrape out the flesh in long strokes; it will pretty much shred itself.

Variations

THAI-INSPIRED LAMB SALAD WITH CABBAGE: To serve over cabbage, thinly shred enough cabbage (whatever kind you prefer) to make about 6 cups. Follow the instructions in the main recipe and simply substitute the raw cabbage for the spaghetti squash. No other changes are necessary.

THAI-INSPIRED LAMB SALAD HORS D'OEUVRE: To serve as an hors d'oeuvre or appetizer, arrange the tender inner leaves of a head of butter lettuce or the tender outer leaves of a head of iceberg lettuce on a platter and spoon the cooked meat mixture into each lettuce leaf. Add the dressing and garnish as in the main recipe. This will serve 3 or 4 people on its own or more if part of a larger selection of hors d'oeuvres.

THAI-INSPIRED LAMB SALAD WITH RICE NOODLES: To serve over rice noodles instead of spaghetti squash, select a thin dried noodle such as vermicelli; you'll need about 6 ounces dried rice noodles to serve 4 people. Refresh the noodles according to the package directions. I find it best to put the noodles in a large metal bowl, cover them completely with boiling water, and let them rest for about 5 minutes, or until they are fully tender. Drain thoroughly. Toss the noodles with the scallions, cilantro, and spearmint and divide them among individual bowls. Spoon the meat on top of the noodles and drizzle the dressing over all. Scatter with the sesame seeds and serve immediately.

Resources

Unlike a generation ago, when the best olive oils and vinegars were hard to find in many parts of the country, today high-quality ingredients are readily found in specialty shops, gourmet food stores, and independent supermarkets. Even so, some of the finest products can still be difficult to get your hands on. That's when it's time to shop online. The businesses listed below provide catalog, phone, and online ordering services. Those with addresses welcome visitors, should you be in the area.

**B.R. COHN WINERY
& OLIVE OIL COMPANY**

15000 Sonoma Highway
Glen Ellen, CA 95442
(800) 330-4064, ext. 124
brcohn.com

Outstanding vinegars and estate olive oil.

CALIFORNIA OLIVE OIL COUNCIL

(888) 718-9830
cooc.com

Information about California olive oil and a comprehensive list of certified producers, with links to their websites. If you don't see a favorite California producer listed in this section, you'll find it at the council's website.

DAVERO

766 Westside Road
Healdsburg, CA 95448
(707) 431-8000
davero.com

Extraordinary olive oils, including an estate oil, vinegars, and other pantry products.

O OLIVE OIL

(888) 827-7148
ooliveoil.com

Outstanding olive oils and vinegars.

OLIO2GO

(866) 654-6246

olio2go.com

Excellent source for the best Italian olive oils and vinegars.

PENZEYS SPICES

(800) 741-7787

penzeys.com

One of the best sources for spices and dried herbs, and the undisputed best online source. Penzeys also has retail stores throughout the country.

ROUND POND ESTATE OLIVE MILL

886 Rutherford Road
Rutherford, CA 94573
(888) 302-2575

roundpond.com

Outstanding estate olive oils and vinegars.

SOULE STUDIO

soulestudio.com

Aletha Soule's gorgeous ceramics, handcrafted in Sonoma County, California, appear in several of this book's photographs.

TERRA SÁVIA

14160 Mountain House Road
Hopland, CA 95449
(707) 744-1114

terrasavia.com

Outstanding estate olive oils and honey; on-site olive mill.

WILLIAMS-SONOMA

(877) 812-6235

williams-sonoma.com

Great source for oils, vinegars (including pomegranate vinegar), and mustards, as well as for cruets, whisks, and other kitchen essentials. There are retail stores throughout the country.

ZINGERMAN'S

422 Detroit Street
Ann Arbor, MI 48104
(888) 636-8162

zingermans.com

Excellent source for Spanish, French, and Italian olive oil, along with rare olive oils from other parts of the globe and artisan vinegars, including Banyuls Wine Vinegar.

Measurement Equivalents

Please note that all conversions are approximate.

Liquid Conversions

U.S.	METRIC
1 tsp	5 ml
1 tbs	15 ml
2 tbs	30 ml
3 tbs	45 ml
¼ cup	60 ml
⅓ cup	75 ml
⅓ cup + 1 tbs	90 ml
⅓ cup + 2 tbs	100 ml
½ cup	120 ml
⅔ cup	150 ml
¾ cup	180 ml
¾ cup + 2 tbs	200 ml
1 cup	240 ml
1 cup + 2 tbs	275 ml
1¼ cups	300 ml
1⅓ cups	325 ml
1½ cups	350 ml
1⅔ cups	375 ml
1¾ cups	400 ml
1¾ cups + 2 tbs	450 ml
2 cups (1 pint)	475 ml
2½ cups	600 ml
3 cups	720 ml
4 cups (1 quart)	945 ml
	(1,000 ml is 1 liter)

Weight Conversions

U.S. / U.K.	METRIC
½ oz	14 g
1 oz	28 g
1½ oz	43 g
2 oz	57 g
2½ oz	71 g
3 oz	85 g
3½ oz	100 g
4 oz	113 g
5 oz	142 g
6 oz	170 g
7 oz	200 g
8 oz	227 g
9 oz	255 g
10 oz	284 g
11 oz	312 g
12 oz	340 g
13 oz	368 g
14 oz	400 g
15 oz	425 g
1 lb	454 g

Oven Temperature Conversions

°F	GAS MARK	°C
250	½	120
275	1	140
300	2	150
325	3	165
350	4	180
375	5	190
400	6	200
425	7	220
450	8	230
475	9	240
500	10	260
550	Broil	290

Index